# *Mirror Image*

Published by:
Crossway Books
P.O. BOX 1123 DUBBO NSW 2830

ISBN   978-0-9757113-7-8

Cover design: Shane Burrell,
Mezzanine Media.
(Newcastle, Australia)

# *Mirror Image*

*You are worth more than you think*

Jenny Marsland

Without the help of the Holy Spirit and my friends this book would be empty pages.

## *I especially want to thank*

Firstly to Brian, my very talented husband, your help in reading drafts and providing technical advice has been greatly valued. Thanks too for all your encouragement.

Jenny Wilson for initially picking this book up and believing in it. I really enjoyed journeying with you.

I would like to thank all my friends who have encouraged me and have prayed for me. A special thank you to Pastor Graham Charlesworth, from Mt Annan Church, for your constant encouragement. Also to David and Rosemary Newby whose understanding of the ways of the Spirit and the timing of God has brought this book to full term.

Adrian and Brenda Bell, Kathryn and Graham Burns, David Henderson, Val Stewart, Sue Peacock, Corinna Promray, Fiona Edwards and Maxine Russell who, not only made order out of chaos, but added special touches to various drafts. Our daughters Jill and Libby for putting up with an absent mum during many long hours at the computer.

To protect privacy in most cases the names used have been changed.

# To Graham

*My only son,*
*who inspired me to push the boundaries of*
*my personal limitations.*
*I will always hold you close to my heart.*
*Love Mum*

God spoke:

*Let us make human beings in our image, make them reflecting our nature.[1]*

Image: replica, counterpart, dead ringer.[2]

We ask ourselves,
Who am I to be brilliant, gorgeous
Talented and fabulous?
Actually who are you not to be?
You are a child of God.
Your playing small doesn't serve the world
There is nothing enlightened about
You shrinking so that other people
won't feel insecure around you.
We were born to make manifest
The Glory of God within us.[3]

# Section One

# Section Two

# Section Three

# Introduction

*Mirror Image* highlights the prison of self-doubt and the dungeon of despair that offence, negativity and adversity plunge us into. These dungeons prevent us seeing ourselves the way God sees us.

*I*magine you and I have been locked in that dungeon. The atmosphere is cold and the darkness is overwhelming. We have always been in this chamber; it is where we live. The years pass, and we are languishing for lack of light.

You begin to wonder what you look like. In your mind's eye you see me describing to you your height, the colour of your hair, the shape of your body. It's only a game; of course you know that. You know I have never seen you, so how can I tell you what you look like?

That night I dreamt that I am in heaven. There, for the first time, I see myself. I am surrounded by pure unadulterated light. I see my beauty, my slender body, free flowing long hair, gorgeous brown eyes and my beautiful smile. God gives me two mirrors, one for you, and one that will remind me of my beauty. As he hands these mirrors to me, he tells me that we can only see ourselves in these mirrors when we hear his voice and read his Word. He gives me a set of keys. These keys unlock our dark room. I wake up and call your name. We grope and find our way to the door. Within moments we walk free.

# Section One

# *One*

# *The Search*

We only get one chance
at life before we
are ushered
into eternity.

*W*e might ask ourselves! "*Who am I really?*" From the moment we are born, we begin the long search to find our identity.

Deep down we know we are not all that we have been made to be. We search frantically to discover ourselves in all sorts of places. Not knowing exactly where to look, we initially depend on our family to tell us who we are. As we grow older we look beyond the identity established by our family of origin and our concept of self becomes driven by image.

We want to be unique. The pressure that society puts on us to become acceptable insists that we be a certain type of person. Appearing beautiful and strong gives instant connection with people. If we have the *right look*, we are accepted straight away. Being accepted gives us worth and significance and is incredibly vital in forming a strong sense of identity.

The world exerts on us an impossible pressure to conform. Fashion magazine are crammed with perfect faces and shimmering straight hair seeking to convince women that they too can be just as beautiful. Billions of dollars are spent on the beauty and fitness industries each year. The beauty salons buzz with frenzy and the gyms and fitness clubs are a hive of activity. Although easily convinced that we can find our identity in external looks, sadly enough, eventually we become disillusioned, since many of us who stare into the mirror of beauty fail to find our true selves.

And what about men? Where do they search to find themselves? Is it not in images of power and strength? Building muscles at the gym, playing (or watching) football, owning a sports car or detonating the enemy in computer games are some of the ways that men spend their time and money creating a self-image. They make the same mistake of pursuing what people admire rather than developing the inner qualities that empower them to live successful lives.

What pressure are you under to be accepted? Where are

you looking to discover your real self? Is it in your work, being a perfect student, having the right size body? Are you looking to find yourself in the music you listen to, your friends, or the clothes you wear?

One of the most common places we look to find ourselves is found hanging on the bathroom wall. It is a known fact that teenagers spend just as much time in the bathroom as they do in front of the television. To the seventeen year old a mirror is just as vital as a mobile phone or laptop computer.

Because other people determine our worth, it is before their faces that we stand in front of the mirror. The big question remains: Is the mirror our friend? Does it tell us that we are beautiful or is it our enemy magnifying our flaws? Deep down the question we are all asking is: Are we good enough to be accepted?

Between the ages of thirteen and thirty I was obsessed with how I appeared before others; I cared deeply about the image I saw when I looked into the mirror. Yet I realised that in looking into the mirror I was searching for something far deeper than a mere reflection of my appearance.

The fairy tale *Snow White* captivated me as a child with the idea that we could find that deeper image by looking into a mirror that has a voice.

"Mirror, mirror on the wall, tell me, who is the fairest of them all?"

The mirror promptly answers,

"You, Oh Queen, you are the fairest."

The queen gave the voice the sole right to determine her value. She was beautiful providing no one surpassed her. Then one day fear and desperation reigned when the speaking voice revealed that someone indeed was fairer.

What mirror are you looking into to find your identity? Do you base your worth on what other people think of you? Do you hang out for compliments and the approval of others? The queen lived eating from the hand of another. But little did she realise that she was setting herself up for failure. One minute the voice in the mirror was assuring her that she was the most beautiful in the land. The next minute, that image was shattered. In all this, the only thing that changed was her perception. Is there a voice standing behind your mirror speaking to your about your worth? If so, what is it saying and how are you responding?

## *Consider*

- What do you think the word *image* means?
- What is the image you hold of yourself right now? Is it mostly positive or negative? Why?
- What gives you worth?

# Two

# *Mirror of Affluence*

*For the world offers only a craving
for physical pleasure,
a craving for everything we see
and a pride in our achievements
and possessions.*
(1 John 2:15 NLT)

# We are imitators

*W*ealth, for many people, often is a powerful line divider for personal worth. Children can make the mistake of thinking that the more material possession they have the more valuable they are.

## Advertising – a deceptive mirror

From a very early age many of us have learnt to measure our worth from the things we own. Owning a mobile phone defines the eleven year old as cool, for those of us who are a bit older, it could be a flat screen TV or mp3 player. Next year it will be something different. No matter what our age, fitting in to what everyone else is doing has become essential to having a good image. The message is clear: you are cool if you look or behave in a certain way.

If we live our lives before the eyes of others, visual imagery will become a major factor in shaping our identity. Advertising constantly tells us that if we want elegance and style (and who doesn't?) then we should wear the latest watch or travel to an idyllic holiday destination. Knowing that we are visually stimulated, advertisers produce ads with a clever sales pitch that convince us that materialism has all the answers. The media and billboards become mirrors that promise to give us the perfection we seek and the power we lack. So we buy that designer label jacket believing it will make us happy, or update our car or invest in the beachfront house in the hope that these things will tell us who we are.

The insidious downside to this trap is that the gaining of wealth creates inner stress. Worry and stress are endemic today. We work hard, go into debt and stay awake at night because we have decided that material things can build our worth. Some of us lean heavily on what we own to make us feel happy, yet the overall sense of emptiness within society is at a perilous level. We have so much, yet we experience so little happiness. "If only I can find what will truly make me happy," we sigh and continue our search. The more we look, the more dissatisfied we feel. Deep within, we know that it is impossible to find our happiness and sense of belonging in things.

## *Reflectors*

Cultural mirrors are everywhere. They insist that we build our self-worth on our external appearance. Of course God wants us to be respectable. He doesn't want us to look and act likes a bunch of dags. There is nothing wrong with using our brains, being wealthy or enhancing our beauty. But if these things tell us a message about who we are and our mirrors become cracked through loss of relationship, job or health, what is left to define us?

Many outside influences shape our self-image. It is what we look to and believe in that will finally determine how we see ourselves. While the advice of people in some instances may be helpful, in other cases it could be harmful. My husband, Brian, and I were driving home late one moonless night and I became aware of the reflectors on the side of the road. Had it not been for the reflectors, and our car headlights shining on them, we would have not known which way the road was twisting or turning. In the same way our faith in others can become a powerful guide as we seek their advice in our journey called life. If we are not careful our dependence on what they say may lead us in a wrong direction. They may even take us completely off track and lead us to unfruitful dead ends.

## Consider

- Why is worry and stress endemic today?
- Are society's mirrors distorting how you see yourself?
- What do you look at to gain or increase your personal value?

# Three

# Mirrors of Fantasy

*We are always looking to find that icon
to reflect back to us who we are
and where we are going.*[4]

23

*E*very little girl dreams of being a princess and every little boy aspires to be a hero. It is instinctive within children to discover their hidden beauty and strength. To help locate these qualities they dress up in superhero costumes. Such outfits allow children to pretend that they are bigger than who they really are.

As we grow older we outgrow our childish ways. With a sudden thump we enter our adult years and life becomes a bit more real and … painful. No longer do we imagine being bigger or better, at least not with superhero costumes. The adventurous spirit subsides as we grind out a living. But there is still a flicker alive in the dying embers of our heart. In our world of Internet blogs and *My Space* we still look for images that make us feel bigger or more important on the inside. Every time we log on and surf the net are we not fishing for something or someone to tell us who we are?

It is in the realm of fantasy that many of us seek to find our identity. In the cinema or in the reading of books we identify with the success in other people's relationships to improve how we feel. We feel good about ourselves when we see someone else displaying love and courage in their relationships. Sometimes we escape into these worlds instead of dealing with our own situations.

## *You saw yourself in me*

We were designed to be rescued from all self-doubt by a Person. Becoming like this Person redefines our worth and enables us to see ourselves clearly. Yet, instead of searching in the right places, we often search for him among the heroes and idols of this world. Recently I had coffee with a friend in a quaint coffee shop. Around the walls were pictures of our past and present icons: Jimmy Dean, Elvis, Bono and others. Quietly spoken conversations faded in into the background as these faces spoke loud and clear. Elvis and Kramer plastered over the walls were saying, "Remember me! I was once your hero; I was the one who gave you significance. You saw yourself in me."

Icons are not only found framed on the walls of coffee shops. They are everywhere. Those of us wanting to conquer wild and dangerous frontiers think of people such as Steve Irwin. Rather than trekking the Himalayas ourselves, we believe that everything he imparted to mankind will also inspire courage in us. For others of us who want to live at high speed and become powerful, we watch Peter Brock who has become a symbol of such living. Our particular hero will reflect back to us an image of the person we want to become.

*Our desperate need is to have our eternal image revealed.*

Let's go back to the coffee lounge. There on the walls I saw a lot of splendour that had faded into the dim lights of yesteryear. These posters highlight our desire to become someone other than we are. Psalm 8:5 states that man is made a little lower than the angels, crowned with glory and honour. That's exactly how we have been made … just a little bit lower than then angels. But often in misunderstanding how God's glory can shape our identity, we often seek a fading glory in the icons of the world.

*"Where there is no vision, the people perish"* (Proverbs 29:18 KJV). We all have a desperate need to discover our true self. Where do we find a mirror that can do that? Is it possible to buy a mirror that speaks to us about our inner worth, significance and value?

Throughout the Bible God has clearly painted a picture of the person we are intended to become. We read that we are the redeemed, a holy priesthood, a chosen nation (1 Peter 2:9) and we are precious, forgiven, washed and sanctified. We are told we are his sons and daughters who are seated with Jesus in the heavenly realms (Ephesians 2:6-7). All authority is ours and we have power over all the works of the enemy (Luke 10:18-19). Yet, how many of these concepts do we really allow to shape us? Many of us find it hard to understand how our identity, as found in the Word of God, has any relevance to our traffic jams and long days at the office. If we don't understand how these concepts relate to our daily lives, we will easily pass them off as irrelevant.

Our value has been firmly established; the highest possible price has been paid. We need to come to terms with our real selves, as God originally designed us to be, so that we no longer idolise those who have what we think we lack. It is only when we stop looking to man, and society's illusions, and look within the heart of God that we will be able to embrace our true likeness. When we start looking for our identity in its original place, we will then find it.

## Consider

- What do you think is the original place of identity?
- Do you search for your identity in the icons of the world?

# Four

## Broken Mirrors

**We gain**
**our**
**worth**
**from others**

27

$\mathcal{W}$e all need to feel beautiful … and many of us work hard to ensure that we do. But sometimes we forget that, even if we are beautiful, not all mirrors give a perfect reflection. A dirty or cracked mirror will prevent us seeing ourselves clearly. Mirrors today are designed without inbuilt flaws; they reflect a perfect image. Years ago when a woman looked into a mirror, rather than feeling better, she felt worse! Such mirrors were made of bronze metal giving a faint blurry affect. How annoying would that be? Imagine how we would feel about ourselves if our only mirror was something resembling the back of a soup spoon which can only give a blurred and distorted reflection. No one likes to see their image defaced or deformed.

Throughout the pages of this book we will look at some of the mirrors that blur our self-perception. Remember, we are speaking symbolically in regards to mirrors. When we want others to tell us who we are, we enter a war zone where anything that speaks about our worth becomes a mirror. From our earliest years we hear messages that make us feel good, and messages that make us feel bad.

## Dazed and confused

Many of us go through life oblivious to the surrounding mirrors that walk and talk and take the shape of significant people: our parents, spouse, children, friends and workmates. If we are treated well by these people we develop a good self-image. But if we are treated badly, even if the innuendo is subtle, our self-image becomes twisted, or worse, grossly bent out of shape. Think for a moment how the mental picture that we have of ourselves becomes distorted through criticism and neglect, or through lies that taunt us if we have been sexually or physically abused.

Recently on Oprah, the program *Challenge Day* was featured. This program is designed to bring healing into the damaged emotions of the teenagers in American high schools. As part of the programme the kids had to walk across a line if they had been humiliated by the opposite sex or sidelined because of either the colour of their skin or the shape of their body. Each time an abusive situation was called out, if the students had experienced that particular humiliation, they had to move from where they were and walk across the line. As the day progressed they discovered that pain, loneliness and confusion was a common feeling among them. Being neither loved nor cherished they had grown up in war zone of verbal and physical abuse where they were terrorised by a barrage of threats. Because of the many years of constant bullying and humiliation they felt they were without a friend in the world.

It has not only physical or verbal abuses that etch a negative self-image. Even the less obvious experiences such as cold shoulders, glances of animosity and doors shut in our face have had a profound influence in shaping us. Not knowing how to dislodge these silent messages many of us have become entangled in their web.

There is within each of us a deep need for others to affirm us. Yet, it is often hard to receive the affirmation we so badly need when we have lived in an emotional war zone. We become cynical and contemptuous, believing if someone is nice to us it is because they want something from us. To receive the affirmation that we need, we first must stop looking into distorted mirrors that tell us we are rubbish.

My dad often said that *beauty is in the eye of the beholder*. This means that something highly valued in the eyes of one person, is discarded as worthless by another. We are both a treasure to God and junk to satan. In God's eyes we are a valued treasure. Yet, to the enemy, we are worthless.

# Power of agreement

Children are born desiring to know who they are. Because their identity is soft and pliable, they become easy targets and succumb readily to bullying and verbal threats. If a child receives a negative message, which is not erased early in life, it can harden and form a negative image. Were you given a negative image concerning your worth when you were a child? Has that image hardened and now forms part of your identity? Do you see yourself as an idiot? Perhaps you see yourself as a loser or someone who is stupid. Has someone told you that you are a nerd, or have they targeted your body saying that you are skinny or fat? Every time we *agree* with these images we move further away from our true self.

> *The thing that matters most is that we see ourselves as God sees us.*

Our negative image becomes the lowest common denominator in determining our worth. If we see ourselves as an idiot we will rarely rise above that image and will behave accordingly. There was a day at school that changed my self-perception in a dramatic way. When I was in third class my teacher caught me talking, and through her words made me feel that I was unintelligent. Up until that moment I had a particular fascination for English grammar. Her off-handed remark smashed my academic mindset and marred my identity as someone who was intelligent. Terrified that other teachers might shoot further arrows into my heart, I never spoke another word in class. My interest in language diminished and I became an average student. For many years I had no idea why I shelved my curiosity in language. I found it really hard to rise above this image. It wasn't until recent circumstances again revealed that I still viewed myself as unintelligent, that I actually had to face this gross distortion. Many of us possess amazing talent, yet our aptitude is hidden by our distorted self-perceptions. Our fear of discovering our beauty and re-building this image into our identity holds us back.

The thing that matters most is that we see ourselves as God sees us. God's Word openly states that we are precious, yet why is it that many of us believe we are of no value? Are we like the queen in *Snow White?* Do we allow people to determine our value? Rather than believing the truth many of us hear that we are wicked and forsaken. Do we believe this lie even though God in his Word clearly says that we are righteous and chosen? Do we live in fear that somehow God will change his mind and say in fact that we are not that beautiful after all?

## Consider

- What do you think a distorted image is?
- Can you think of ways that abuse distorts our image?
- Who or what do you think might be hidden mirrors in your life?
- How much of your image has been shaped by negative experiences?

I blended in
but
longed to be
noticed
as
someone who
was
special.

# *Five*

# *Blinded by the Lie*

*The god of this age has blinded
the minds of unbelievers,
so that they cannot see the light.*
(2 Corinthians 4:4 NIV)

$\mathcal{M}$any of us are living way below our true potential. Throughout our lifetime we have believed lies that have shaped our self-worth. Lies such as: God doesn't really like me ... he doesn't know I exist. ... if he loved me things wouldn't be so tough ... I would have more money and more friends ... I would have a better job and live in a better area.

Some have believed the lie that in order to be successful they need to earn more money, to be significant they need to be married, or to give up their addictions they need to find happiness.

Such lies convince us that we will never become the person we dream of being. I'm not talking here about becoming a supermodel or a millionaire. I believe our deep desire is to overcome life's circumstances. We can only do this by believing the truth about ourselves.

From an early age my self-image was shaped by a myriad of lies. As a result I grew up feeling part of the furniture; I felt that nothing really special set me apart from the five point four billion people on the planet. I blended in but longed to be noticed as someone who was special.

When I became a Christian, much of what I read in the Bible seemed too distant from where I lived. The claws of self-hatred had dug deep into my heart. I could not see beyond how others were treating me. If I didn't matter to people, then in my mind, I didn't matter to God. I had no idea how to translate his love into my everyday living. Although God became a passion in my life, I still didn't know who I was, nor did I understand the depth of his feeling for me. I remained captive to negative thinking. It was during this time of doubting that God placed within me a desire to find out why I discredited myself so much.

He led me to understand that our present identity is closely connected to an event that occurred at the dawn of time and is only briefly mentioned in the Scriptures. To address the issue of identity we first need to revisit a garden where our ancestors, Adam and

Eve, stood before a forbidden tree.

## Hidden danger

God knew of the hidden danger within the tree. As a mother would warn her child against running in front of a truck, so God warned Adam and Eve of its danger. *"For when you eat of it, you shall surely die"* (Genesis 2:17 NIV). Because God loved Adam and Eve, he did not want them to experience evil or even know about it. However satan, who knew that the tree would open their eyes to his dark kingdom, described God as a cosmic killjoy who was trying to keep something good from them.

The slithering snake carefully crafted a lie that lured Adam and Eve down from the height of glory into the depths of shame. Rather than coming out with a blatant lie, he twisted the truth and appealed to Eve's sense of desire. *"You will become like God, knowing good and evil"* (Genesis 3:5 NIV). The ironic truth is that "becoming like God" would prevent God being the only one who would tell them a message about their worth. Instead a mixture of pleasure and pain (good and evil) would have power to tell them who they were. God was shielding them from this mixture that would snuff out the light in which they lived.

> *The claws of self-hatred had dug deep into my heart. I could not see beyond how others were treating me.*

Eve, seduced by a lie, was now hooked. It is in the realm of desire that a lie gains its greatest power. Seduction comes to us dressed in the very things we want. We cannot be seduced by something that we are not already looking for. A man cannot be seduced by a woman if he is not already seeking for someone to fill his empty heart. What we often forget is that the very things we hope will fill our emptiness can become a source of bondage in our lives. A defiant attitude … a marital affair … a food addiction … an obsession with the Internet may all seem to be the answer to our needs. Adam and Eve wanted something other than God to tell them who they were. This *other than God* would become the enemy to their souls.

I wonder how life would be for us if Eve had kept her desires in check. Adam and Eve put us in a position where we are now unable to see our worth. In this realm of darkness our growing desire to find our value intensifies. We have become susceptible to all sorts of voices that claim to have the exact picture of our likeness. Befuddled we listen to all of them.

> *Down through the ages both God and satan wrestle over the heart of man with the purpose of shaping our identity.*

In not having the original copy of ourselves, we build our identity tenuously on the opinion of others. The broken pieces of our identity have become like the red and yellow building blocks we used to play with as children. As we build our identity on beautiful images our enemy, through negative words and unfortunate circumstances, destroys our masterpiece.

When Adam and Eve ate of the apple, the spiritual climate changed from that of life to death; from a beautiful garden to a battlefield. We were born into this war zone, and in this atmosphere we search for life. To find the life we are looking for, each of us will need to fight our own personal battles.

Jesus plummeted the depth of hell and took back the keys that gave the enemy a right to destroy our identities. Even though the war over our identity has been won by Jesus we still need to choose who will determine our worth. The person we give the exclusive right to shape our identity wins our daily battles. We can give that right to the enemy of our soul, and we will never like ourselves. Or we can give that right to the lover of our soul, the one who originally made us. He alone sees our true worth.

My aim in writing this book is to alert us to the truth that our spiritual heredity is a sought after treasure. Down through the ages both God and satan wrestle over the heart of man with the purpose of shaping our identity. As a result of Adam and Eve's actions, we are still trying to fit together the pieces that went missing on that day.

## Consider

- Why is our identity connected to the garden?
- What was the hidden danger in that tree?
- Eating of the fruit of the tree would destroy Adam and Eve's ability to see themselves as his image-bearers. Explain.

To discover
our
true worth
we
have to be willing
to change
the
way we see
ourselves.

# *Six*

# *Adventure of a Lifetime*

*We now have this light shining in our hearts, but we ourselves are
like fragile clay jars containing this great treasure.*
(2 Corinthians 4:7 NLT)

# War declared

*A* war has been declared over our identity. Are we conscious to the fact that our true eternal image is constantly under attack? It is easy to recognise when a car has been bombed in a terrorist attack, but harder to perceive are the missiles sent on a daily basis to damage our image. The enemy's warfare strategy is to make the woman feel ugly and the man weak. Once an image is programmed in, the enemy then sits back and allows that image to do its work of destruction. Craig Hill says, "If satan is able to establish his images of identity and destiny in your life he then has set up a system of governing your life that more or less runs itself and requires very little maintenance or service on his part. It is an effective scheme of destruction in your life."[5] To ensure the lie takes a firm hold the enemy orchestrates circumstances that make us feel worthless and insignificant. Once these situations begin to affect our identity, he then confirms these images with messages that we are:

- unforgiven
- unprotected
- unloved
- unrighteous
- insignificant
- irrelevant

Jesus came to intercept this downward spiral by programming good healthy images into our identity. God knows that these positive images can make us internally strong and will become a source of protection. To instil images of value and significance, we need to receive God's goodness.

To receive God's goodness, he takes us on a journey with him. Up until the time I was married, I had lived in the same house and spoke to the same people. Nothing much had changed in my world. But in opening my heart up to God, and allowing him to pour his goodness into it, my life was expanded in unimaginable ways. My journey with God has taken me to places I never dreamed possible. I never thought that I would live in a third world country nor did I imagine living in the city where I would be exposed to the cruel side of addictive lifestyles; or in a small village at the base of a mountain. I never dreamt that I would write a book, or get a chance to shine God's light into the dark places of broken hearts. I never thought I would be betrayed or offended in the ways that I have, or experience the pain of adversity that has touched my world. The journey of the heart has taken me into situations of perplexing difficulties and long stretches of apathy and loneliness. The journey has taken me into the wild frontiers of my heart; the barren places, the hard unyielding places of doubt and fear; of desire and despair.

## *Hidden treasure*

Throughout my journey God has been looking for the treasure that he placed within me; my faith in his goodness. God's goodness is his glory, and it is the measure that we trust in his goodness that our glory is restored. There has been many times in my life where God's goodness has been hidden behind doubt and unbelief.

> *The Bible is full of imagery that decribes our worth.*

Just prior to moving overseas to live in a remote village in the South Pacific, so that Brian could teach in a Bible college, I found it hard to see God's goodness. My friends would joke that we would be the last missionaries there because the natives would eat us. Little did they realise that I had read many books in my early days of conversion about missionaries who had been eaten. Over the years this fear slowly consumed me until the time came where it appeared that it would became real in my circumstances. The day before leaving, a friend gave me this reassuring word from God.

"My dear little sheep, we have travelled such a long way together haven't we? You have followed me over many rough places and at times you have wondered why your shepherd would lead you across such dry desert places or up such steep mountainous tracks. But my loved one the high places are so refreshing once the arduous climbing is over and I your shepherd can delight in relaxing with you as you feed on the lush of the mountain top, far away from predators, secure in my presence, totally protected. But now the time has come for me to take you into an unknown place, unknown to you, and already I sense the tension within you as hundreds of the enemy well aimed darts of fear assail you. Be still and trust me totally. I know exactly where I am taking you and I know too the wonderful outcome of the circumstances ahead. I am your shepherd. I will carry you forever."

> *God desires we follow him into circumstances where he is able to give us a deep clear view of our worth.*

## *Alone and without help*

Within a week of receiving this word, Brian and I and our three small children arrived in the Solomons Islands. On arrival I had no idea of the changes that I would have to make. To reach our new home on the isolated peninsula, we had to travel for many hours on rough seas. It was late at night when we finally stepped off the small cargo boat onto the wharf. As the rain poured down we were greeted to the sound of some of the most harmonious voices

I had ever heard. Following the indigenous people to our house with only our lanterns giving light, I wondered how the previous missionaries survived. I was out on my own with very little support. My family and I were totally isolated, with no medical facilities and no shops.

In those early days of settling into a new way of life, I felt desperately alone. Memories of my care-free life back in Australia faded into the background as my new surroundings became the backdrop for an adventurous nightmare. Very early I learnt that a pig had more value than a woman. Everything that gave me value in Australia diminished before my eyes. The weather was hot and stifling and the days were long and monotonous. The food was bland and boring, and I was without help.

No longer distracted by the buzz of life I became acutely aware of my reactions and the attitudes causing them. Through hot, long and boring days God orchestrated situations that revealed deep hidden doubts concerning my worth. It was when we were nearing the end of our time there that God clearly showed me that he brought me to the Solomon Islands so he could conqueror my heart and reveal its true worth. In fact, by the time I left, I felt God's presence in extraordinary ways. His constant presence has become part of my new image in which I have lived for the past fifteen years.

Looking back over my time in the Solomon Islands I realised that, although my life lacked the normal comforts that I previously enjoyed, I had been given everything that I needed to handle my new environment. Each time we open ourselves up to change and we step outside our comfort zone, we will discover that God has placed within our heart exactly what we need to overcome our particular problem. To withstand the strong winds of adversity God has given each of us his strength, determination and courage. To be able to withstand the arrows of offence he has made us merciful, gentle and kind. These things enable us to overcome every obstacle and ultimately reveal God's glory. So that we might connect our situations to eternity and discover God's perspective he has given us a reflective and insightful heart. We can lose everything that gives us our outward identity, such as our looks, wealth, prestige, and reputation, but we can't lose the true essence of who we are on the inside.

*Where there is no vision [no redemptive revelations of God], the people perish"[6]* The Bible is full of imagery that describes our worth. We are loved, forgiven, accepted, chosen, valued, washed, (clean from the stain of our sin) sanctified (considered holy) and set apart (to live for God alone). The enemy desires to destroy these images, so he orchestrates circumstances that will make them appear illusionary. If we hold onto the enemy's construed imagery, we can get stuck in a rut. A rut elongates and deepens as it furrows through our entire lives. Perhaps you think the same thoughts each day going over that devastating event that occurred fifteen years ago? We can get very comfortable in our ruts because they provide a sense of security. There is a sense of safety in what we can predict. To discover our true worth we have to be willing to change the way we see ourselves.

> *The concept of being happy and fulfilled originates in the heart of God.*

Up until the blind man followed Jesus out from his familiar surroundings, he had not been able to see.

> *When they arrived at Bethsaida, some people brought a blind man to Jesus, and they begged him to touch and heal the man. Jesus took the blind man by the hand and led him out of the village. Then, spitting on the man's eyes, he laid his hands on him and asked, "Can you see anything now?" The man looked around, "Yes, he said, "I see people, but*

*I can't see them very clearly. They look like trees walking
around." Then Jesus placed his hands over the man's eyes
again. As the man stared intently, his sight was completely
restored and he could see everything clearly.*
*(Mark 8:22- 25 NLT)*

To have his sight recovered, the blind man had to follow Jesus into
the unknown. It was there Jesus was able to touch and heal his
blindness.

Everyday circumstances become the perfect opportunity for
God destroy the lies that we have believed and reveal his goodness.
Jesus came to give an abundant life. Yet, we can't enter that life
if we aren't prepared to see ourselves differently. We must open
ourselves up to the possibility of discovering that we are greater
than what we think. An adventurous life demands risk.

Adventure isn't hanging on a rope
off the side of a mountain.
Adventure is an attitude that we must apply
to the day to day obstacles of life -
facing new challenges,
seizing new opportunities,
testing our resources against the unknown
and, in the process, discovering our own unique potential.[7]

## *Opportunity for change*

Facing new challenges, seizing new opportunities, testing our
resources against the unknown all sounds pretty scary to me. Yet,
we are made for adventure and we have what it takes to endure our
journey. Even in our scariest of moments, God is with us and he
becomes our shield of protection.

Katie's resources were tested against the unknown when

she faced a medical challenge. She discovered that through her trial she was bigger on the inside than what she originally thought. When I first met Katie, she was in the worst of her nightmare. In seeking God he told me that he was taking her on an adventure that was to reveal her true worth. This adventure had many terrifying moments for Katie. She tells:

"Three years ago I was diagnosed with a genetic neurological condition. God has used an illness to help me understand the depths of His love for me. In what appears to be a hopeless situation in which I could not cope, God has shown me He can help me. Through experiencing His strength and His peace he has given me the courage to go forward. I can't handle this life. It hurts too much and without him there are too many disappointments. He has shown me that my value has everything to do with being loved by Him. My value is not in what other people see in me. His love overcomes everything and is constantly overcoming my difficulties." Katie discovered that her value wasn't to be found in her talent, her brains or good look, which she has a good supply of. Her value lay in being loved by God and receiving his goodness.

> *Jesus, who has come to restore our vision, desires to touch our sight not once, but many times.*

## Love affair of the heart

Trials are an invitation to break free from our narrow self-perceptions. God desires that we follow him into situations where he can reveal his goodness. He desires to show us that there is nothing that can remove his love from us.

I love adventure and have had plenty of it. As a child, I had no idea of my worth, so I began searching for traces of my value in all sorts of places. I couldn't even begin to imagine that

I was beautiful. I spent most of my life thinking I was ugly. I was never ugly, but being treated badly made me think I was. Further to that, my responses to how I was being treated made me feel dreadful. God made each of us with amazing qualities. Often we don't realise our true value because we have never seen just how beautiful we are. Perhaps no one has ever told you that you have worth. Instead people have made you doubt yourself.

Recently Brian and I were at an AFL football match in Melbourne with Graham our son, and Zephyr, his girlfriend. As I walked into the stadium I sensed that God was going to speak to me. I was totally unprepared for what transpired. The issue of my fear of heights was raised. Well, guess where we sat. That's right – the very top level. Looking down I felt giddy. As I turned my thoughts toward heaven I realised God was asking me to face a lie that I had believed about myself for over thirty years. Although it would be difficult to disclose all the details of the conversation, God told me why I had become susceptible to the lie. He then spoke into my heart and destroyed the lie with the truth.

Our worst fears cannot separate us from God's unfailing love. You see, many of us have deep doubts concerning his love. These doubts prevent us becoming all that God has designed us to be. To prove that nothing can separate us from his love, God uses our difficulties and everyday obstacles to reveal his constant love and presence. Often these situations become worse before they get better. If we are patient, these adverse situations can become the perfect climate into which we discover something new about the depth of our worth.

Think about the real person you are – when you are by yourself. Have you allowed an unfortunate situation or personal weakness to become a barrier, preventing you from understanding your worth? Have you become burdened by issues of depression, loneliness, shame, frustration or fear? Maybe you felt like your whole world ended when you experienced a particular tragedy.

At that time did you come close to God so he could reveal your true worth? Did your weakness give God a chance to reveal his magnificent grace and power in your life? God sees you according to the strengths he has placed in you. Before God you are eternally precious and no amount of personal weakness or physical limitation can erase this truth.

Are you currently going through a situation that is causing you to doubt yourself? Be encouraged! God desires to dismantle the negative messages preventing you from seeing your value. He desires that you come in your brokenness so he can tell you the truth concerning your worth. Be willing to face your challenges. They are designed to reshape the way you see yourself. What you are going through right now has a purpose to build courage into your spirit and help you realise that there is nothing that has the power to separate you from God's love. God desires to show you the plans that he has for your life. He desires to reveal further aspects of his conquering Spirit placed within you.

We don't have to prove ourselves. Our sense of wholeness can't be found on the outside; it comes from within. Our worth surpasses our greatest bank balance and highest accolade. It surpasses our greatest gifts and talent. Although these things are great, they are far too small to define us. Our value surpasses our scars of the past, our deepest trouble and the most painful affliction. Our self-worth is inherent within us. It is dependent on being made in God's image and receiving his goodness. It rests in hearing God's voice and embracing his love. Once we discover God's goodness we won't need to frantically add anything into our lives to make us valuable.

The concept of being happy and fulfilled originates in the heart of God. Eternal life is an encounter right now with the Creator God who personifies fun and excitement, and delights in revealing his strength in our weakness, his voice in our silence; his peace in our storms and his love in our conflicts. The Christian life is the

48

best life possible; full of fun and spontaneity. But most of all the Christian life is a love affair of the heart. To become our lover, God invites us on adventure.

Have you got your bags packed? Are you ready to embark on a journey of your lifetime? Would you like to discover the treasure that has been placed inside your heart?

## *Consider*

- How do you see yourself?
- How do you think God sees you?
- Have you followed God into an adventure that has revealed the depth of your worth?
- How can difficult situations become an adventure with God?

Designed to outlast
the
test of time,
our identity
as
reflectors
will never be erased.

# Seven

# *Kharakta*

*Within the council of the Godhead, He cried out,
"I ...the living God ...alone...the one who is ...
I shall have a counterpart!"* [8]

*T*o recognise a counterfeit, we must compare it to the original. God has placed within us the pieces that we are looking for. These pieces are found in our eternal blueprint. When your mother first held you she had no idea she was holding much more than nine months of intense planning and dreaming by our creator. Many of us are unaware of our unique blueprint - God's specific image and plan that he has for our lives. You see, our true image was formed at the beginning of time when God breathed on man. *"The Lord formed the man from the dust of the ground and breathed into his nostrils the breath of life, and the man became a living being"* (Genesis 2:7 NIV). We originate from the breath of God and the kiss of heaven. Our true identity is not physical but spiritual.

## *The perfect mirror*

To aid us in our search, God holds up before us a mirror. Each time we open the pages of the Bible we look into this mirror. This mirror is perfectly clean and can never be shattered. Standing the test of time it will continue to reveal our likeness throughout eternity. Every time we look into this mirror we will see that we are righteous and blameless While standing in front of this mirror we will see that we are the counterpart to God; the pinnacle of creation and have been handpicked to become like him (Ephesians 1:4). This mirror highlights our uniqueness.

> *You are **beautiful,** my darling, as Tirzah,*
> *Lovely as Jerusalem,*
> ***Majestic** as troops with banners.*
> *Turn your eyes from me;*
> *they overwhelm me* (Song of Songs 6:4-5NIV).
> *Arise, come my darling, my beautiful one*
> *and come with me ... in the hiding places*
> *on the mountain side.*

*Show me your face, let me hear your voice,*
*for your voice is sweet,*
*and your face is **lovely.***
(Song of Songs 2: 13-14 NIV)

Have you ever considered how extraordinarily beautiful and majestic you are? Your eyes overwhelm God. He desires to hear your voice and see your lovely face. There has never been, nor will there, be another person exactly like you.

Designed to outlast the test of time, our identity as reflectors will never be erased. As we reflect him we will show the world what he really looks like. The Greek word for *image* is *kharakta* and means character [9] and carries with it the idea of "absolute sameness."[10] As we allow God's character to determine our worth, we become more and more like him. Our ability to reflect God is not seen in how we look or what we own, but in how we respond to the challenges of life. To become our true selves, we need to place firmly in our imagination the following images.

> *To recognise a fraud, we must have the original.*

We are:

- forgiven - we won't be punished
- protected - we won't be harmed
- chosen - we won't be discarded
- needed - our "used by date" won't expire
- loved - we won't be devalued
- righteous - we won't be condemned

# Cracked mirror

Our dilemma is that the enemy has a mirror too. He holds up the mirrors of injustice, trouble, suffering and offence. Many times, by staring into these wrong mirrors, I have become locked up in a place of darkness where I have been unable to see my beauty. Have you been there? Do you think you are ugly because you have a physical flaw, or a poor aptitude, or an inability to succeed? Maybe you are unable to make friends or hold a conversation. The enemy of our souls will highlight these inadequacies as often as he can. Just as the queen heard a voice behind her mirror, so the enemy speaks to us behind these mirrors. Each time we hear his voice, we doubt ourselves.

Whenever we feel ugly, unwanted or worthless, it is usually because we have been looking into one of the enemy's mirrors. If we look long and hard into these mirrors we can find ourselves captive to images that simply are not true.

Rapunzel is a fairy tale of a young girl who became locked up in a tower with an old witch. The young girl is in fact very beautiful, but the old witch continually tells her that she is ugly. As with all fairy tales Rapunzel carries with it an analogy to the human heart. The story isn't really about a girl in a high tower. The story shows us that we too can live in captivity to our own self-perceptions. Rapunzel's captivity is really the fear of her own ugliness. Rapunzel's freedom occurred when she saw her prince charming standing at the base of her tower. When, in the eyes of her rescuer, she saw that she was beautiful she was freed from her cruel misconception.

We are called to be a light in a dark world, but we can't be that light if the opinions of others have caused dark shadows to fall over us. The enemy will always be working hard to keep our true identity in the dark by flicking up before us mirrors of trouble, offence and negativity. Satan wants to destroy our identity and delights in making us feel insignificant, unwanted and unloved. If he can confuse us he will have an advantage and prevent us from winning the particular battle that we are facing.

To prevent us from understanding our true identity, the enemy tells us that we are:

- unforgiven - we will be punished
- unprotected - we will be harmed
- rejected - we will be discarded
- not needed - our "used- by- date" will expire
- unloved - we will be devalued
- unrighteous - we will be condemned

Many years ago I too had become locked up in the tower of my own imagined ugliness. This negative image prevented me from living life to the full. This ugly image had become lodged deep in my heart where no one could see. It gripped my soul like a vice. No amount of self-improvement seemed to change the way I saw myself. God knew the depth of impact the lie was having in preventing me accepting myself. He was waiting for me to seek him. Eventually I became desperate to find out who I really was. Through a friend, God intervened with the truth. He said, "My precious daughter, I am the master jeweller. I choose with great care. Once I have chosen my jewel, I polish it upon my sleeve. Then I facet the stone to reflect the brilliance of my light. Once cut, I polish that gem with love and persistence. My child, you are a chosen jewel being polished and facetted to a mighty brilliance by my hand. My precious child, I love you. Rest in my love and shine for me." These words smashed those negative images and set me free by helping me to see myself though his eyes.

We need the light of God to shine when the voices of the world cast shadows over our worth. His light, that penetrates into the dark areas of our heart, reveals the truth and sets us free from our dungeons of self-doubt.

The light that reveals our worth, however, threatens the enemy. He hates it when we finally see our value. So to prevent us seeing clearly, he distracts us with other lights. These lights may be a philosophy, a science religion or a cult where man is god. Body, Soul and Spirit festivals highlight that we are spiritual beings; they also draw attention to the many religions claiming to restore the light for which we search. But the luminosity that we are looking for cannot be found in crystals or tarot cards.

> *"My beloved is fair and ruddy, the chief among ten thousand."*

The light that is able to give insight is exclusive to the eternal God, *"O Lord my God you are very great: you are clothed with honour and majesty, You cover yourself with light as with a garment"* (Psalm 104:2 NKJV).

## Brilliant light

Nicky Cruz escaped a cold dark prison of self-doubt when he caught the penetrating gaze of God's love in the life of David Wilkinson, a street evangelist. In a recent series of meetings here in Australia Nicky told of how satanic chants from his mother caused him painful humiliation. To hide his shame he left home at an early age and became the leader of one of the toughest street gangs in New York City. He discovered a new approach when preacher David Wilkerson heard the call of God and walked onto the Mau Mau turf in New York City with the indelible love of God. Fearlessly, David endured spits in the eye, slaps across the face and death threats. With a will as strong as iron he penetrated the hardened heart of gang leader Nicky Cruz with the love of God.

Nicky, looking for his identity in bravery, discovered that love made David not only fearless and determined, but also armed and dangerous. Those were the qualities that Nicky wanted to be known for. Nicky like a "caged animal" was terrified of that which he had never experienced - love. David Wilkinson didn't go into the Mau Mau turf to find out who he was. He was on a mission to shine light into a group of boys who were on trial for murder. As a result, Nicky discovered that rather than being satan's child, he was passionately loved by God and was destined to speak to millions of kids about the life transforming power of the gospel.

Nicky shows us that we can escape our dungeons of despair by looking beyond ourselves to a God who is passionate to restore our identity. Just as Nicky and Rapunzel were freed from their distorted images when they gazed into the eyes of their loving rescuer, so we too must gaze into the eyes of our rescuer if we are to have our self-image transformed.

Jesus is the One who sees your true worth. He is dazzling and is described in the Song of Songs as *"My beloved is fair and ruddy, the chief among ten thousand."*[12] Jesus stands at the base of our high tower waiting to rescue us from the cruelty of a distorted self-debasing image. Our Saviour is light personified. *"His face was like the sun shining in full power at midday."*[13]

Jesus has a passion to restore 20/20 vision concerning our worth. The Word of God is a perfect mirror that gives us an opportunity to change our mind about ourselves. It will show us who we truly are. It is possible to discover our worth, and it is my desire to show you that you can know your true value right now. But first we need to remove the unbelief preventing us from seeing Jesus.

In sending his precious only Son, God devised a counter attack to rescue us from the cruel tyrant that holds us captive. Jesus died a gruesome death and gave up his own life to snatch us back from the enemy and restore to us our true worth.

Jesus, who has come to restore our vision, desires to touch our sight not once, but many times. Jesus has special skill in opening the eyes of our heart. He does this by telling us the truth. Receiving revelation and insight from Jesus destroys the entire array of mirrors that seek to sabotage our identity.

*To aid us in our search God holds up before us a mirror.*

The enemy is nervous that we discover our eternal blueprint. He strategically distracts us with the mirrors of the world. To fulfil his purpose satan uses the hidden mirrors of:

- rejection
- offence
- intimidation
- trouble

These mirrors trap us by demanding we conform to their perception of us.

As each mirror is lifted before you, smash it so that you will never have to believe its message again. In their place, take hold of Jesus, the faultless mirror. Allow him to tell you who you are.

*"The righteous are as bold as a lion"* (Proverbs 28:1 NIV). As we smash the distorted mirrors, the Lion of Judah will rise up in us and we will become outrageously confident. If however we fail to smash these mirrors we won't fully understand the power within us and we will remain just like the kitten, focused on the moment, small, and vulnerable to life. For those of us who want to find our true selves, it's time we allowed the weak and timid kitten inside to become transformed into a triumphant lion.

## Consider

- What are some of the mirrors the enemy flicks up before us?
- How do they affect our identity?
- Do you see yourself as a light bearer?
- Mention briefly at least three things that God's Word tells us about our worth.

To overcome our
desire to please people,
we first need
to
overcome our
fear
of rejection.

# Eight

# Do You Like Me?

*Forget what people think about you –*
*otherwise you will be locked*
*into a realm of fear.*
Anon.

*A*re you struggling, feeling frazzled and burnt out? Are you exhausted, overwhelmed, confused, uptight or anxious? If you are, you are not alone. Many people are struggling with such an array of emotions because they live with a haunting fear of rejection. We are on a search for our significance. One of the most sought out places we seek to find our worth is in the approval of others. We feel valuable when we are loved and appreciated by our friends and family. I have yet to meet a person who delights in being rejected. Rejection rates as one of our greatest fears because it cuts into our deepest basic human need of belonging. We all need to feel a sense of belonging. Since rejection fails to meet this need we often become an easy prey to the habit of pleasing people.

## *Crisis of identity*

The Bible is our identity textbook. As we open its pages we enter a supernatural realm where God whispers into our hearts and opens his arms to embrace us with love and acceptance. Within the pages of the Bible there are many accounts of people who knew their true identity. We read of their amazing exploits as they pushed back every obstacle that sought to destroy their worth. Although most knew who they were, there were some who didn't know their true value. To varying degrees these people lived with a fear of rejection. We see God shining his torchlight into Saul who was such a person.

Samuel came to anoint Saul as king, Saul answered, *"But am I not a Benjamite, from the **smallest tribe** of Israel and is not my clan the **least of all the clans** of the tribe of Benjamin? Why do you say such a thing to me?"* (1 Samuel 9:21 NIV). Saul was chosen to be king yet he held an inner identity of being the "least of the least." This crisis of identity set him up for failure. Saul gained his poor self-worth from his family. He grew up belittling himself because his family felt weak and insignificant. Yet this didn't seem to bother God who called Saul to be king in the very midst of his struggles.

God tested Saul to determine if his identity had improved. At first the tests were simple and easy and Saul passed admirably. But then the tests became more complex as the pressure to please the crowds mounted before him. It was at one of these times he miserably failed. Sadly he laments, *"I cared more about pleasing the people. I let them tell me what to do."*[49]

When our self-image is small we often rely on the opinion of others to build us up. If we believe that man holds the mirror to our true image we will become addicted to his approval. Saul felt that he couldn't obey God and still be accepted by the people. He feared being rejected by man and lost his position as king. If we seek the approval of others to determine the basis of our worth we build our lives on the very words that cost Saul his kingdom. That is a great price to pay for a brief moment of acceptance.

> *Knowing that we are sons and daughters who are eternally accepted is a vital key to recovering our lost identity. .*

## War zone of compromise

To overcome our desire to please people, we first need to overcome our fear of rejection. Because some of us still struggle with a poor self-image, just like Saul we often ignore God and become addicted to pleasing people. When we live for the approval of others we enter a war zone of compromise. In our own personal walk with Jesus do we follow the crowd above doing what Jesus says? "Everyone else is doing it," is the common catch cry that justifies much of our behaviour. We trade in our bona fide selves for fleeting moments of acceptance. We compromise our standards, beliefs and dreams and camouflage our real selves so that we can be squeezed into various moulds that the world shapes for us. If we depend on the world around us to assure us of our value, then being accepted by our friends will become a number one priority. It is not only the youth that mimic each other in order to be accepted. As we grow older we also experience pressures to conform. As a result we all pretend to be more or less than we really are. This makes us weary.

## *Invisible weights cause profound weariness*

> *When we measure our lives against what other people have, or are doing, we can become depressed.*

Sally became weary searching for her worth. She says, "I met Mark thinking he was going to save me from this harsh, cruel world and look after me for the rest of my life. No one could convince me that I was a beautiful person on my own merit. I needed someone to define me and make me feel whole. In choosing Mark to be that person I threw away my freedom. I found that I had to do a lot of things to please him. He criticised me when I wanted to do the things that I normally did. I love spending time with people but Mark wanted all my time to himself. Even though I tried so hard to make him happy, I felt like I was carrying a huge weight. I had little energy and was continually agitated. I couldn't even concentrate at work. One day I realised how much of my true self I had thrown away just so he would like me."

Weariness comes into our lives, not only because of what we do, but because we care deeply what others say about us. Our need to be accepted creates a profound weariness that settles on and covers our hearts like a thin cold mist. Like all mists, we feel ever so tiny droplets resting on our emotions long before we actually understand that it is a weight.

Weights in the gym are used to build muscle. If, however, we carry weights in our handbag or brief case, our arm would not develop muscle but become tired. Whatever we do just so others can accept us becomes abnormal weights that cause us to be tired and depressed.

How can we discover our true worth if we have to do what everyone else is doing? Wouldn't it be great if we could make choices that honour God and not be worried about people's responses? Unfortunately this is rarely the case, so we become fearful and choose instead to please our friends. Not fully appreciating our worth, many of us become weary as we seek the affirmation of others. We burn ourselves out when we put too much emphasis on pleasing people.

If we measure our lives against what other people have, or are doing, we not only burn ourselves out, but we can also become depressed. When I was in the Solomon Islands, I found it really easy to compare my life with the lives of my friends in Australia. They had everything and I had what I considered to be very little. They seemed to be enjoying life to the full and I was sitting on an isolated peninsular eating rice and fish. One day I was complaining to Jesus about my dilemma and he surprised me with his answer. He helped me to see that even though it appeared that I lived a solitary life, he had none the less, chosen me to be a reflector of his glory. He told me that we needed "time out together" so he could conqueror my heart. Much of what he did with me in the Solomons Islands became foundational in shaping who I am today.

## Driven desire

Satan recognises that if we don't hanker after acceptance from others his hold on us is weakened. His clutch is loosened when we choose to please God above pleasing others. Knowing we are totally accepted by God protects us from our own need for position or title before man.

Our constant desire for approval wears us out and ultimately prevents us believing God. Jesus asks us, *"How can you believe if you accept praise from one another, yet make no effort to obtain the praise that comes from the only God?"* (John 5: 44 NIV). The Pharisees wanted man's approval. They blew their trumpets loudly, prayed in public and gave their money so they could be noticed by man (Luke11:39-52). Jesus warned us not to be like the Pharisees whose motives were mixed with a desire to outwardly please God, by doing what he required, but inwardly they really wanted man's approval.

We constantly rob ourselves of our individuality when we want to please people. "Fitting in" has become the god of our age. God doesn't want us to find our significance through the eyes of others. He desires that we look into his eyes and discover our worth. God didn't use the gingerbread cutter to make us all look the same. A billion little clones made to reflect the same aspect of his character was not what God had in mind. He made us unique. If we understood the power of our uniqueness we wouldn't compare ourselves with others.

> *Jesus walked free from the need to be accepted by man because he knew who he was.*

A.W. Tozer recognised this weight of expectation that others insist we carry. "The burden borne by mankind is a heavy and crushing thing."[50] Yet Jesus gently invites us to drop our weights and come to him. *"Come to me, all of you who are weary and carry heavy burdens, and I will give you rest"* (Matthew 11:28 NIV). Jesus' invitation is given to all of us who are tired of living in war zones, searching for identity and worth by trying to please others. Are we growing tired in our search for approval from others? We can know by estimating the extent to which we live to gain their acceptance. When we depend on others to meet our deep need for approval, weariness envelopes us like a thick blanket and paralyses our spirit with apathy.

Jesus walked free from needing approval because he knew who he was *"The Son is the radiance of God's glory and the exact representation of his being"* (Hebrews 1:1-3 NIV). Jesus knew he had infinite worth. He was not only equal with God, he was God. Yet as he walked on the very dust that he created, he didn't flaunt his deity, nor did he demand that people worship him, but instead he positioned himself without rank and status before man.

> *We trade our bona fide selves for fleeting moments of acceptance*

Jesus enjoyed a deep sense of belonging. Secure in being a loved Son, he was not distracted by self-esteem issues but held a constant gaze toward heaven. Never doubting his identity Jesus remained unmoved in the midst of great difficulties. He easily performed miracles despite the watchful and disapproving eye of the Pharisees. Jesus walked free from the need to please people and he offers us that same freedom. Jesus had an amazing impact but never once did he seek to build a reputation for himself or place of status. If Jesus didn't look into warped mirrors seeking the praise of man neither ought we.

A Vietnamese proverb says, "When a tiger dies he leaves behind his skin, when a man dies he leaves behind his reputation." Our need to be known and recognised plays a big part in forming our identity. Do we gain our significance by being known for what we do and where we live? Why don't we allow Jesus' death to become the basis of our worth? Why is it that we don't base our true value and significance in being known and accepted by God?

Knowing that we are sons and daughters who are eternally accepted is a vital key to recovering our lost identity.

God made us in his likeness and not in someone else's. It is not before man we are to live but before God. This does not mean we live the life of a recluse. On the contrary it is vital to connect with each other. Even though Jesus was misunderstood by people he also had many friends. However, when in the company of his friends, he still did not try to please people. He was connected but never once did he compromise his relationship with his Father to gain approval.

> *Our search for significance will end as we fall into God's loving arms. .*

We are not created to live according to our perceived need of man's approval. You see if we live before man with the need to perform and succeed it will be impossible to become who God made us to be. All of this begs the question, why are we so afraid of being unique?

## *The key to freedom is to know who you are*

Each time we are rejected and we take our wounds to Jesus, he reassures us of our eternal acceptance. There is no situation we can face that can mar our identity with the label, "rejected." As we repent of trusting in man, our focus on ourselves will lessen, and we will enter profound rest. As we learn to receive love and attention from the throne room, we will no longer feel so frazzled, and our image will no longer be blurred through that thick fog of desire for the approval of man. As we are refreshed by Jesus' words our emotional exhaustion will cease. Our search for significance will end as we fall into God's loving arms. This may sound a bit daunting, but truly it is where power and protection lies. It is in the very place of having no reputation before man our need to defend our worth lessens.

When we understand our divine design we will be secure in our uniqueness, we will walk in rest and naturally reflect to others our true identity.

## Consider

- What are invisible weights?
- *"Jesus made himself nothing."* What does this mean to you?
- What should our reputation be based on?
- Do you compare yourself with others?
- Has your desire for acceptance propelled you into the arena of pleasing people?

Those of us
who doubt ourselves
go to bed each night
tending our wounds.
God's army
loses ground
on a daily basis
and
the casualties
some
days
are
in their millions.

# Nine

# Idolatry Blurs Vision

*So what do you think?*
*With God on our side like this, how can we lose?*
*If God didn't hesitate to put everything on the line for us,*
*embracing our condition and exposing himself to the worst by*
*sending his own son,*
*is there anything else he wouldn't gladly*
*and freely do for us?*
*And who would dare tangle with God by messing with one of*
*God's chosen?*
*Who would dare even to point the finger?[14]*

## Offence belittles what God has esteemed

"You never listen to me," blurted Ruth as she stormed off into the restaurant. Inside she appeared calm and friendly but I knew she was upset. As I drove her home that night, I raised the issue of her earlier outburst. As we talked I could almost visibly see the Holy Spirit expose and then clean off a distorted image that tormented Ruth.

"I could never get my Dad's attention," lamented Ruth.

"He was always distracted doing other things,"

"How did this made you feel," I gently asked.

"I felt unimportant and that I am a nuisance to him. I have to speak so fast, because I have to get out everything I want to say before he shuts me off," she said.

Ruth had been busily telling me about her day when I became distracted. This unbeknown to me, reminded Ruth of all the times when her Dad had ignored her. Ruth lived with a message that she was worthless. Many times she tried to push down these feelings, but eventually everything surfaced.

## What is offence?

We all need to feel loved and accepted. It is part of our identity. The enemy is always seeking ways to destroy our worth, and one of his favourite ways is to make us feel rejected. One of the greatest ways the enemy can make us feel rejected is to offend us. Offence has been described as: "the act of **attacking** – or assaulting to offend." The aim of this attack is to cause the victim to respond in "**anger, resentment**"[15]

Jesus describes the kingdom of God like a never ending party. The bridegroom is with us and it is time to celebrate. We have been lifted out from our pit and placed on a royal seat. We are entitled to be treated with respect and honour. Yet we live right in the middle of the enemy's territory and our assailant, the devil, wars hard to destroy our identity. The war starts long before God has a chance to tell us the truth concerning our worth.

## War begins in childhood

Children have feelings and are aware of their surroundings. Because children have little resources to express their feelings when inwardly hurt, they easily become offended. Recently I learnt that my brother Gary had feelings that he couldn't express. As a result he grew up believing that I was a threat to him. I didn't find out about this until recently. He relates the incident. "A couple of months ago while enjoying a wonderful family reunion; Jen and I were talking about old times. I mentioned to her an event that I still remember as clearly as though it happened yesterday. At the time I was about three and half, Jenny was ten months younger than me. We were with our Mum who was going to a corner store in Moree. We left by the back gate taking a short cut through a small paddock. Suzy, who was the baby, was in the pram (an old cane basket type that few would now remember) and I was riding on the front, hanging on to the handles used to push the pram. Jen was walking. On the way home from the shop, Mum stopped pushing the pram and asked me to get down and let Jenny on. I recall asking why we both couldn't share the ride, to which came the reply, 'You're old enough to walk all the

> *Even though people may say very hurtful things, ultimately it's not their words but our confidence in what they say that has the power to distort our image.*

73

time now, it's your sister's turn to ride the pram.'

A couple of years later we were playing a game inside the house. Suzy and I were running really fast down the hall sliding on the polished wooden floorboards. We were heading toward the double glass doors but just moments before we came to them we stopped and disappeared into another room. Jenny, who was following us, didn't stop but continued straight on out through the glass doors and landed on a huge pile of newly raked catheads. As she came into the house crying, rather than feeling sorry for her, I felt smug and strangely vindicated." Unable to express his feelings, Gary became suspicious of me. He feared that I would take from him the privileges that he enjoyed.

Do you have memories of being offended when you were a child? Have you found it hard to forget the past and move forward because a negative impression concerning your worth has been imprinted in your heart? The enemy's specific purpose in provoking offence is to fuel self-doubt. Every time we are offended the self-doubt in us deepens.

## Doubt

We don't wake up one morning with an overwhelming sense of self-doubt. Doubt begins almost unnoticeably. It starts with a sarcastic remark or an ignored phone call. A series of small offences can make us irritable and touchy. Little by little we become more cautious and self-protective. A sharp criticism can take from us all hope of being beautiful and significant and can send us plummeting into the pit of despair. When arrows of rejection, blame, or criticism hit and then wound our heart, we scramble back into our self-made cave for protection. To defend ourselves we build high walls to guard our emotions. We long to be known but we refuse to be honest and reveal ourselves. The message has become so confusing that our only option is to stay behind the safe confines of ambiguity.

For those of us who were attacked at an early age offence becomes one of the enemy's most successful strategies to further damage our image. Have we become discouraged because others have implied that we are not good enough? If we have grown up doubting our worth we will find it hard to like ourselves. You can't like someone you doubt. If we despise ourselves how can we expect others to love us?

*With incredible precision Satan aims his arrows of offence with the purpose of destroying our image.*

When we are offended by those who we love and respect, we become deeply hurt. Broken trust and betrayal can alter our feelings from that of inner wounding to anger. Do any of these emotions describe how you feel?

- Annoyed
- Angry
- Infuriated

*"Why has your heart carried you away, and why do your eyes flash?"* (Job 15: 10-11 NIV). Has someone made you angry and now you have become trapped by depression and self-pity? Ultimately satan wants us to be angry; he pushes our limits so that we end up hating ourselves and disliking everyone around us. Have you noticed that enemy is always throwing out his bait hoping we will bite? But we really need to stop and ask ourselves, "Why is it that we become so easily angered?" Has someone told us, either verbally or with their body language, that we have no worth and that we are insignificant? If we know in our hearts that we are significant, why has their message offended us?

Self-doubt becomes an invisible magnet attracting people

> *Many Christians severely doubt their worth*

who will also doubt us. In the past I had a lot of doubt concerning my worth. Although I thought it was okay that I secretly doubted myself, I didn't think it was okay when other people doubted me. Even though at times I thought that I was loser, it hurt me when I found out that other people thought that same thing. When other people have offended me, it is usually because they have agreed with something that I have already believed about myself.

## Take Responsibility

If we have become offended, maybe it is time that we stop and ask ourselves some questions. Why have we put so much confidence in their words? Has the arrow of offence hit a spot exposing something that we have already believed about ourselves? Has our interpretation of their words caused us pain? Eleanor Roosevelt says that no one can make us feel inferior without our permission. These messages can even be received from people who we deeply love and trust. In the place of greatest trust we can be wounded. *"The wounds I was given at the house of my friends"* (Zechariah 13:6 NIV). Satan works hard to sever connections between family, friends and workmates. But primarily he seeks to offend us so that we are unable to see our true worth.

## Idolatry

We will never understand the full depth of our worth if we gain our identity from man. In fact, gaining our self-worth from man is the most basic form of idolatry. "If a relational message of identity and/or destiny is conveyed to me by another person, and I simply receive it as truth without checking it out with the Holy Spirit, then I have just made that person a god in my life. I have entered into idolatry."[16] A relational message speaks into our identity and worth. In placing our trust in man, we actually place our trust in idols. *"Those who cling to worthless idols forfeit the grace that could be theirs"* (Jonah 2:8 NIV). Our idols are not real, they are phantom like. The words of man are but a breath, and this is why we are told to *"stop trusting in man, who has but a breath in his nostrils, on what account is he?"*(Isaiah 2:22 NIV).

If we understood the strategy behind the offence we receive, we will be able to rise up and defend ourselves in a way that no one becomes hurt or wounded further. Retaliation has caused many casualties on the battle field; the more people we hate, the greater the enemy's victory.

It is vital that we understand that the ploy of the enemy is to destroy our true worth; and he uses the trust that we have in people to do this. We destroy our worth when we trust people. *"Cursed is the one who trusts in man, who depends on flesh for his strength"* (Jeremiah 17:5 NIV). When we believe man in such a way that affects our identity we actually place ourselves under a curse. The Greek verb for *curse* is *anathematizo* and means "devoted to destruction."[17] God gives us a choice. We can either trust him to shape our worth, or we can trust man. If we depend on man to form our identity, we will base our self-worth on images that are formed by lies. It was the enemy's ploy at the garden to ruin our worth, and now he fights even harder to fulfil his mission. Our true worth lies in being made in God's image. We mustn't forget just how precious we are, nor should we forget that at the core of our being we are righteous (2 Corinthians 5:21) and are seated with Jesus (Ephesians 2:6). We are no longer covered with shame but rather God sees our beauty and declares us unique. We are his loved and chosen jewel who is beautiful with no flaw (Song of Songs 4:7). We have stolen his heart. God keeps this vision of us continually in his thoughts.

To overcome offence we must be confident in the image that God has of us. If we don't rely on God and his opinion, we set ourselves up to be ensnared. God's purpose is to ensure that nothing has power to affect our self-worth in a negative way. The more able we are handle offence, the more confident we will be.

If we destroy our doubts, and reaffirm our worth, we will be patient when the arrows of offence are aimed at us. *"Better a patient man than a warrior, a man who controls his temper than one who takes a city"* (Proverbs 16:32 NIV).

## Consider

- How do we help others in the process of destroying our worth?
- Has someone wounded you and now you find it hard to forget the past?
- The enemy seeks to offend us so that we are unable to see our true worth. Have you seen this happening in your life?

# *Ten*

# *Intimidated*

*They sharpened their tongue like swords
and aim their bitter words like arrows.*
*(Psalm 64:3 NLT)*

*Bullies push and shove
their way through life* [18]

*W*ords have great power and I will never forget the first time I felt their force. I was only five at the time and we were standing just outside our back door in Moree. A whole bunch of younger kids and I were trying to decide whether or not there was a God. We couldn't agree on an answer and, frustrated with the indecision, I was surprised to hear my self boldly declare that if there was a God I would believe in him. As those words tumbled out of my mouth that day they enabled me to see myself as one who was bold and destined to know God.

The next day, feeling very much alive and desiring to be adventurous, my brother Gary, sister Suzie and I were playing in our front yard. We became interested in the council workers who had opened a manhole so that they could work on an underground pipe. Because of the danger involved they told us to go away. In our curiosity, we refused. They tried various tactics to send us on our way, but to no avail. Probably in their frustration one of the workman said that the devil was going to come up from the ground and "get me." Fumbling for the courage that came so easily the day before, I ran, not only from them, but from the devil that I imagined was now after me.

The words that are spoken to us have a profound effect in forming our identity. Often, instead of realising their power, we either brush off what is said to us as irrelevant, or we inwardly run. The enemy's ultimate aim is to dominate the way we think about ourselves. The first step he takes to do this is to intimidate us. The definition of *intimidation* is to *"make timid and to **scare**"* and *"To **discourage** from acting by threats or violence."*[19] Concerning my own brush with intimidation, my question has been, "Why didn't the man alert our mother to the fact that we were being a nuisance?" The front door was only a metre or two away. Interesting, isn't it, that instead he reprimanded us with a threat of violence. This violence was not of a physical nature but of a spiritual nature. The picture he painted in our minds made us feel that we would be attacked by a spiritual entity that somehow seemed more powerful than the man himself. This idea threatened our future (I only wish I knew at the time that the devil had been defeated and has no power to harm us).

Up until the force of those words impacted me, I had lived an uneventful life. But then everything changed. My vivid imagination locked me into a negative mindset from which I could not escape. Rather than feeling bold and confident, I felt anxious. The fear, created by those words was so great, that I ran off, taking with me a distorted self-image. From that moment on, rather than seeing myself as one who was bold and confident, I shrunk from being the tallest to the shortest. I became obsessively self-conscious and everything seemed to be against me.

> *It is only as we destroy negative imagery concerning our worth that we will be able to see ourselves as God sees us.*

God gives us indescribable worth, and he expects that we show others that they too have worth. The best way satan can stop us from doing this is to use the sharp edge of a tongue to defile our minds with negative imagery. We can't love others when our minds are filled with depressing thoughts.

## *Overwhelmed*

We are involved in a full-scale war. Peter warns us, *"Your enemy, the devil, prowls around like a roaring lion looking for someone to devour"* (1 Peter 5:8 NIV). The word *devours* means to *"eat greedily"*[20] *and* carries with it the idea of being overwhelmed or overpowered.

I lived most of my childhood overshadowed with a pervading sense of evil. Whenever I read fairy tales about giants I felt overwhelmed. It wasn't so much the size that frightened me. Their death-threatening words became the source of my fear. Fairy tales such as *Jack and the Bean Stalk* struck terror into my heart. As Jack ran from the giant I could feel my own adrenalin racing. Little did I realise, metaphorically speaking, that giants are people or circumstances whose purpose is to intimidate. Over time I came to realise that by using words to belittle, giants aim to mess with our identity by making us feel small inside.

## Jezebel - a giant

Elijah discovered a giant in his midst when he called a showdown on Mount Carmel and challenged the god Baal which had infiltrated the land. In calling on the true God to send fire from heaven, just under a thousand Baal prophets realised that their god was powerless and Elijah's God was supreme.

Jezebel was a prophetess of Baal and on hearing of her god's defeat was furious and sent a note to Elijah threatening to kill him. In reading the note, Elijah's focus shifted. Where he had previously made a lifestyle of seeking wisdom, he forgot to check this matter out with God. Instead he swung the pendulum across to man's opinion. Elijah's eyes shifted off the all-powerful God who sent fire from heaven and focused on another type of destructive fire – one sent from hell. Jezebel's vicious words became poison tipped arrows that endangered his future. Deeply depressed, he ran for six weeks until he came to the safe haven of the mount of Horeb.

> *The fear, created by those words, was so great that I ran off taking with me a distorted self-image.*

It was there in the cave, while catching his breath, God appeared to Elijah with a question, *"What are you doing here Elijah?"* (1 Kings 19:9 NKJV). Elijah spilled out his complaint and laid his fear before God. God responded to Elijah's predicament by reassuring him in a gentle voice (1 Kings 19:11-13). God's words breathed life back into Elijah's spirit and destroyed the fear of death brooding in the contours of his mind.

It is common to feel discouraged. But often we refuse to go to God and tell him our feelings. Instead we run away. Why is it that we easily forget the Scriptures that say, *"the Lord is my helper, I will not be afraid. What can man do to me?"* (Hebrews 13:6 NIV).

When confused, God gently asks us this question.

*What are you afraid of – or who?*
*Some man or woman who'll soon be dead?*
*Some poor wretch destined for the dust?*
*You've forgotten me, God, who made you,*
*Who unfurled the skies, who founded the earth,*
*And here you are, quaking like an aspen*
*Before the tantrums of a tyrant*
*Who thinks he can kick down the world.*[21]

In other words, God is asking us to consider who are we when we say that a man has more power than him? Normally we compare our size with what or who we are standing near. Stan is a short man. But it isn't until Stan is standing conversing with Bill, who is a tall strapping man, that I realise just how short Stan is. If I stood near a skyscraper and looked up, I would feel tiny in comparison. In a similar way, words can tower over us and make us feel very small. If we forget God's size and power then everything could lose its perspective. We are not to measure overpowering words or intimidating threats according to their size but according to God's Word. Through his Word, God lifts negative images off our minds and re-interprets our circumstances with his truth.

When arrows, carrying threats of punishment, wound our hearts let's not forget their source. Even in the midst of turmoil, the question remains: what and whom are we running from?

> *But what will come of their tantrums?*
> *The victims will be released before you know it.*
> *They're not going to die.*
> *They're not even going to go hungry.*
> *For am God, you're very own God,*
> *Who stirs up the sea and whips up the waves,*
> *Named God-of-the Angel-Armies.*
> *I teach you how to talk, word by word,*
> *And personally watch over you.*[22]

Have you believed a lie that you are, at this present time, running from? If so God would ask each of us again, *"Whom have you so dreaded and feared that you have been false to me and have neither remembered me?"* (Isaiah 57:11 NIV)

## *Words are the enemy's weapons*

God created the world through the spoken word. Our words are creative. It is part of being made to be like God. In their creative ability lies their hidden danger. We are all taught the dangers of walking in the middle of a busy three-lane highway but rarely are we taught the creative power and potential danger of the spoken word. The tongue is *"restless and evil, full of deadly poison"* (James 3:8 NLT).

The tongue is so powerful it can create an atmosphere of life or death (Proverbs 18:21). *"Kind words heal and help, cutting words wound and maim."*[23] Scathing words make us feel condemned, unwanted and ugly. By allowing such words to affect us they can appear real in our circumstances. When destructive words penetrate our soul our outlook becomes tainted and our thinking becomes bleak and gloomy to such a point where we grope about in sheer darkness.

*"It only takes a spark, remember, to set off a forest fire. A careless or wrongly placed word out of your mouth can do that."*[24] Every day at work, at home and in our relationships we experience derisive words. These words can become so gigantic in our minds that they can prevent us seeing God and his purposes.

Brian and I were driving to our friends place for coffee when I noticed that my leg was unusually itchy. In reaching down to scratch it I realised that the problem was a scaly and bleeding mole. We rushed straight to the doctor's surgery. On examination I was warned that the mole could be life-threatening. The mole was removed at once and sent for testing. The doctor felt it his duty to warn me of its danger and he had me dead and buried even before the results had come back.

> *To destroy all the effects of intimidation we must take a firm hold of the truth.*

The doctor could have made me feel small and helpless. At that point I could have taken off in my imagination and had myself attending my own funeral! As I sat before this bearer of bad news, rather than feeling overwhelmed, I remembered God's promise to *"bless me and not to harm me and to give me a future and a hope"* (Jeremiah 29:11). Needless to say, the doctor was perplexed at the peace in my life. When the negative results came back I realised that had I not been so aware of God's presence, the doctor's words could have penetrated my spirit and created a deep fear in my life.

# The battleground of the heart

We live in a war zone and the target is our heart. There, hidden in our hearts, are buried both good and bad perceptions concerning our identity. This mixture has a profound influence in determining our worth. Before I knew how to check things out with God, I doubted myself severely. In response to some of the arrows that I received I made some really bad decisions. I still live with a harsh reminder of some of those choices. Life is a hard teacher when we fail to put God above man. Have you been like me? In response to a person's belittling words, have you made unwise decisions that have actually brought you into a realm of greater danger?

I know of young people who have signed out of school because the peer pressure had become too great; I know others who have become addicted to food and alcohol because of their feelings of worthlessness. Marriage commitments have been easily discarded in the divorce courts because neither party were able to communicate their true feelings. Perhaps, as a child, you were told by religious people that God was angry and that the devil would get you. Perhaps you were physically or emotionally abused and now you have withdrawn and become disinterested in your true calling to be like God.

Are you currently running from a situation that you find hard to face? Are there people and circumstances still appearing bigger in your mind each day? God desires that we face our giants and reject their messages. As we do this we develop a pure heart devoid of all negative imagery concerning our worth.

*"Blessed are the pure in heart, for they shall see God"* (Matthew 5:8 NIV). Pure hearts remain uncomplicated in times of difficulties and uncontaminated in a world full of negativity. To develop pure hearts we need to remove all negativity from our thinking. Making a conscious effort to do this prevents us from making stupid decisions. It gives us the ability to think clearly and

act wisely.

To destroy all the effects of intimidation we must take a firm hold of the truth. Truth has the ability to release peace. The more truth we sow into our lives the more courageous we will be. Because the enemy is seeking to overpower us, it is vital that we have a good supply of truth in our arsenal. By using this truth we can resist the devil and destroy his lies. We need a militant attitude as we rise up and throw down toxic thoughts that defy God's opinion of us. It is only then that we are able to grow into the destiny that is ours.

## *Consider*

- Are you discouraged?
- Is there a person or situation threatening you?
- How do you deal with a person who is using threats to control your behaviour?
- Have you the inner resource to withstand their attacks?
- Do you draw from the strength that God has given you?

The true test
of
self-acceptance
is
our ability
to
deal with offence.

# Eleven

# The Crossroads

*I will lead the blind by ways they have not known*
*Along unfamiliar paths I will guide them.*
*I will turn their darkness into light before them*
*And I will make their rough places smooth.*
*These are the things I will do:*
*I will not forsake them.*
*(Isaiah 42:16 NIV)*

## Strategy of warfare

*You shall **be protected from the lash of the tongue** and need no fear when destruction comes. You will laugh at destruction.*
(Job 5:21 NIV)

*E*lijah, deeply wounded by the power of Jezebel's tongue, found a safe haven in the arms of God. The New Living Translation interprets *"will be protected from the lash of the tongue"* as *"you will be safe from slander"*. The Amplified Bible translates this as *"you will be protected from vicious gossip and live fearlessly through any catastrophe"*. You *shall be hidden from the scourge of the tongue* (Job 5:21 NKJV).

God is able protect us. But to do this he needs our cooperation. He can only defend us if we destroy the lie feeding the gossip and slander. We must seek him for the truth. The truth will form a positive image. As we hold that image in our hand we are then hidden from the power of the tongue and are lifted out from our deep waters. In our place of safety, all the weapons formed against us will be destroyed (Isaiah 54:17). The perfect image that God has of us becomes a shield deflecting weapons formed against us. Circumstances will no longer empower our feelings.

*Anger, sorrow, fear and resentment are four signposts that will reveal we are at a crossroad.*

It is our ability to deal with offence that indicates the level to which we have adopted God's view of us. The more we understand our spiritual DNA, the less we will be offended. God has a strong desire that we rise up and destroy every negative word spoken against us. We can't overcome an offence if we neither understand our true worth nor understand how God feels about us. It is at the crossroads that we discover both our worth and God's ability to redefine our self-perceptions.

> Go stand at the crossroads and look around
> Ask directions to the old road,
> The tried and true road. Then take it.
> Discover the right route for your souls.[25]

This old road is also known as the eternal paths. As we walk in these paths, God's image will be restored back into the deepest part of our being. Every door that has prevented us seeing our worth will be unlocked and a perfect self-image will be restored. If we walk in these paths we will find rest for our souls.

## The old road restores a perfect self-image

Every road has an intersection where decisions are made concerning direction. Within our hearts there are also places where decisions are made. It is important that we recognise when we come to a crossroad. Anger, sorrow, fear and resentment are four signposts that will reveal we are at a crossroad. A crossroad is any place where our ego has been wounded and we have become angry. It is any place where we need to ask the question, "Are we going to get over our hurt or are we going to turn down a sidetrack and be offended?" Usually our response is something like, "I will show them that I am not to be messed with." Do you go to bed angrily nursing your wounds? Do you feel sorry for yourself? Then it's time to make a decision.

If someone can wound our ego and cause us to be angry, we give a space for the enemy to gain entrance. "*A fool gives vent to his anger, but a wise man keeps himself under control*" (Proverbs 29:11 NIV). We can keep ourselves under control by pausing at the crossroads and asking for direction.

## Prisoner of war

When I was about six years old my younger sister and I went to live in the city with my aunt and uncle. At first I felt very special but after months of not seeing my parents I felt abandoned. The rationale of a young mind concluded that I must have been very bad to deserve such treatment. This idea crushed my sense of worth. By the time my parents and I were re-united, I was convinced that this was the truth. For years I was miserable, frightened and angry. I began to eat the enemy's food of negativity. I was easily intimidated and failed to see my true worth. I was constantly discouraged and could not love others the way God did. It was many years later, whilst alone with Jesus, that he showed me I had become a prisoner of war. In a single encounter I was shown what this meant. We become a prisoner of war when we:

- refuse to forgive those who have hurt us
- believe the lie that was imparted about our worth
- agree with the devil about the offender
- think negative thoughts about the person who hurt us
- bow down in our mind to the image of them hurting us
- shut them out of our lives cherish the hurt and hold it close to us.

## The crossroads

If we refuse to confront our pain the offence will become lodged in our hearts. It is vital therefore that we deal with offence as soon as we are aware of the signposts. The crossroad brings us to a place where:

- decisions are made
- truth is received

- stains are removed
- message is reframed
- hidden lies are brought to light.

The crossroads brings us to a place where we decide which message we are going to believe about ourselves. Instead of believing that we don't belong or that we are unlovable we can ask God how it is that he sees us. Every time we do this we will be surprised at his wonderful vision of us.

God "*reveals his thoughts to man*" (Amos 4: 13 NIV). When God asks us to walk on the old road, he gives us direction by speaking to us. One day I was standing at the same old crossroads, ready to take a detour down the enemy's track. However, this time I looked to Jesus and I asked for his image of me when I felt abandoned. He spoke these words into my heart, "I am always thinking of you, and I would never abandon you. I love you so much; you have incredible worth to me. I am always listening out for you to speak to me. When I hung on the cross, I was thinking of how close you would be to me one day. I was thinking how for you I would be separated from all love and go into the depth of hell and take back the devil's keys that gave him access to your life. I was so happy that he would no longer have the pathway to your life because you belong to me. I thought of the moment when you would finally understand the reason for my death. No one has the power to stop me loving you. I am totally free to dance with joy over what you mean to me."

*Lies aimed at our identity can penetrate our spirit leaving deep wounds.*

Although offence never comes to us nicely wrapped in a presentation box, I believe it is a gift that God wants us to unwrap.

Underneath the wrapping, (whatever form it takes) an opportunity exists for God to reframe the offence and remove the stain. Removing the message of offence requires that we search out the truth about our worth. This truth becomes a shield that protects our heart.

## *The crossroad reframes offence*

Our identity is made up of value, significance and belonging. If any of these three areas are attacked we will be offended. If a key person has made us feel unimportant, and we don't let the offence go, we can open ourselves up for others to deepen that wound. Because we lack understanding, we forget that we have great worth and throw our value out as if it is totally insignificant. *"Therefore my people will go into exile for lack of understanding their men of rank will die of hunger and their masses will be parched with thirst"* (Isaiah 5; 13 NIV). Gaining understanding from God prevents us believing terrible things about ourselves.

Have you given up completely because your heart was wounded many years ago? We are conquerors. But we can't conquer what we don't confront. We often react when we have been reminded of those times when we have previously been hurt. These situations reinforce old messages.

Reframing a photo cuts all the unnecessary bits out of it. Reframing focuses on the main character. Likewise reframing the message that offence brings cuts out all the rubbish that the enemy used to taint our image. We can reframe the way we see ourselves by taking responsibility for our feelings. In order to cut out all the rubbish, God desires that we tell him how the offence made us feel. It is only as we tell God our feelings that he can then unravel the lies energising our pain. It is only as we get God's opinion that we can eliminate the messages sent to destroy our image.

Counting the sand on the beach is an impossible task. Just one handful holds thousands of tiny grains. God has many thoughts about us which have the ability to destroy the lies we have believed. In fact Psalm 139 states that God's thoughts about us outnumber the grains of the sand on the beach. And it is precisely these thoughts that become part of the table prepared for us in the presence of our enemies (Psalm 23). Right in the middle of our conflicts, in the very presence of our offender, Jesus sets a whole table of truth before us. Yet we have to go to that table and decide whether or not we will believe the truth. As we begin to understand how God's Word relates to us personally, we then are able to see our true worth. While previously we may have been blind to our value, God heals our sight by teaching us to believe good things about ourselves. Although these things may appear too good to be true, nonetheless, they are real.

*"The right word at the right time is like a custom-made piece of jewellery"*[26] A couple of years ago while in a Bible study I was praying for Ashley. Ashley had recently joined the group because her brother, who had been dramatically changed by God's love, brought her along. As I was praying I heard God tell me that he loved her with a passion. Later that night, Ashley told me that a friend of hers (obviously upset with her) said that very day that she hated her "with a passion." As I shared God's timely word for Ashley, she was able to reject the enemy's lie and see herself as lovable and valuable. If you check negative messages out with Jesus and discover the hidden lie targeting your true identity, its power will be dissolved. It is possible to destroy every lie that has given you a wrong view of yourself.

When we bring our broken image to God, he can restore it. God has a perfect picture of us in his heart. It is our job to find that picture. When the image that God has of us becomes valuable to us, we will guard it with great care. This doesn't mean that we live from the realm of our ego. It means we live from the realm of the supernatural by gaining and valuing God's opinion. Our identity is to be protected as we would guard our most treasured possession.

*"He reached down from heaven and rescued me: he drew me out of deep waters. He rescued me from my powerful enemies; from those who were too strong for me. They attacked me at a moment when I was in distress; but the Lord supported me."* (Psalm 18:16-24 NLT)

## Stain remover

Dealing with offence at the crossroads removes the stains on our lives. Stains are unsightly and often are impossible to remove. When our children came home with fresh stains on their clothes from the rough and tumble of a sports day at school I would remove those stains instantly. But if some of their clothes were washed before I noticed the stain it became part of the image for that piece of clothing. The stain marred what otherwise was perfect.

Lies aimed at our identity can penetrate our spirits leaving deep wounds. The longer the lie has been believed, the deeper the image will have been planted, and the stronger the hold it will have on our lives. While standing at the crossroad God will shine light on these stains that have been buried deep in our hearts. Uncovering the source of the lie involves recognising how it previously affected our self-perception. If we take responsibility and challenge those negative messages, their power will be dissolved.

When a negative picture of ourselves looms large within our minds, we can shrink that image by challenging our thoughts. In the movie, *Honey I Shrunk the Kids* the children become the size of ants and the parents become giants. Someone's opinion of us can loom so big in front of us that we can feel very small by comparison. If we feel powerless to confront that image we can reduce its size by getting God's opinion.

## The truth makes us strong

As we confront and discard the myriad of lies that have formed negative images in the past, we can then rise up and become the people who we are made to be. As we face our fear we come to realise that God is the only one who can really show us who we are. He alone holds the key to our identity and has everything we need to feel significant, valued and accepted. His presence reveals our blueprint and helps us to understand that "*the one who is in us is greater than the one who is in the world*" (1 John 4:3-5 NIV). In times of trouble God highlights the wrong messages that we have believed about ourselves and replaces those messages with truth that is based on the original plans that he drew up for our lives.

> *The Lord God is my strength, my personal bravery*
> *and my invincible army;*
> *He makes my feet like hinds' feet*
> *and will make me to walk*
> (*Not to stand still in terror, but to walk*)
> *and make (spiritual) progress upon my high places*
> (*of trouble, suffering or responsibility*)!*" [27]

Daniel believed the truth and was delivered from the jaws of the lions. Just as Daniel could have been torn apart by lions but "*no wound was found on him because he has trusted in his God*" (Daniel 6:23 NIV), so too we will be protected. God has given us truth to believe that will set us free from all our doubts. Often we know this truth in our mind but our hearts fail to agree with this truth when we are facing our foe. To bring our hearts and minds into agreement, God teaches our hearts to come into agreement with the truth in our minds. In this way, that truth is able to affect our emotions. As we believe the truth we will turn to look for our enemies, who sought to destroy our self-worth, but we will not find them. The enemy can nudge us with his insinuations, annoy us with insults or even push us to react with his intimidations but, with God's opinion of our true worth, our armour will become so thick that the enemy won't even make a dint in it.

## Consider

- "It is only as we get God's opinion that we can eliminate the messages sent to destroy our image." Explain how we gain God's opinion.
- Explain how the crossroads have affected you today.
- Why is it that we can react so bitterly to a situation that is of little significance?

# Twelve

# Fog Lifted

*We don't yet see things clearly.*
*We're squinting in a fog,*
*peering through a mist."*[28]

God uses adversity to shape our character. But the enemy takes the tool of trouble and forms it into a mirror. Rather than shaping our identity, this mirror deforms it. If we allow circumstances to determine self-worth we open ourselves up for the enemy to harass us.

My family and I live in a valley and during the winter months a misty fog settles onto the road, especially late at night. We can barely see the street lights and have to drive slowly.

Fog can become to us a nebulous sense of doubt that settles on our minds and prevents us seeing clearly. The fog lifts when we remember that we are:

- forgiven
- protected
- chosen
- needed
- loved
- righteous

From time to time life presents us with normal challenges. Although these challenges may be part of our daily lives, they still can affect us. Many teenagers severely doubt their worth when they are rejected or misunderstood. Many parents equally doubt their worth when their teenagers rebel. If we don't believe that we are righteous then trouble will shake our confidence and confuse our identity. This confusion often remains long after the storm of adversity subsides. Consider these scenarios. Suppose your boyfriend or girlfriend breaks up with you. Instead of getting over the hurt quickly, the message that you have no worth seeps into your heart. Or perhaps you lose your job. Instead of picking yourself up quickly you may now feel that you are insignificant and that your skills are not needed. These are not the messages God wants you to hear. You have worth and are lovable no matter how others treat you. God sees you as having profound significance whether you have a job or not.

The pressure of adversity can become so great that something in our attitude will have to shift. We need to change the way we see ourselves to survive the trauma. Harsh environments give us the opportunity to re-assess the way we see ourselves. If we are going to make a difference, we have to be different. We can't be different if we complain and think negatively, nor can we make a difference if we are too hard on ourselves. If we fail to adjust our vision the enemy will interfere with our identity.

Paul's faith in Jesus made him a wanted man. From the shores of Judea to Jerusalem a death warrant was issued against his life. He suffered much, "in *great endurance; in trouble, hardships, imprisonments and riots, in hard work, sleepless nights and hunger*" (2 Corinthians 6:4-5 NIV). He gained the skill of subduing his enemy by placing all the lies concerning his worth under his feet. By learning to use weapons of righteousness, he became confident in the midst of great trials. *"We are ignored, even though we are well known. We live close to death, but are still alive. We have been beaten but have not been killed. Our hearts ache but we always have joy* (2 Corinthians 6:9-10 NLT). Paul didn't allow circumstances to define his worth but rather he depended on the indwelling presence of God to reveal the glory which he had been made to reflect. Having such a mindset prevented life touching him on the inside.

Stephen, the first martyr in the New Testament, had a deep understanding that his worth was connected to being loved and forgiven. This, in time, had huge impact on Paul (who at the time of Stephen's death had a vicious attitude towards the Christians and was known as Saul). Paul (who later was dramatically transformed and became a brilliant light) witnessed the peace and glory on Stephen's face as he beheld a vision of Jesus moments prior to his death (Acts 7:56). Stephen had in no way allowed Paul to speak a message to him concerning his worth, but trusted himself to a faithful creator Are we like Stephen when life's situations are condemning us?

What is life like for you? Do you see your potential for enormity or have you grown up believing that you are inferior to others and unworthy of God's love? Have you heard the message that you really don't deserve to succeed and that you are incapable of greatness? When we accept these messages our subconscious mind takes hold of these images and brings them into reality. Our self-perceptions formed by these beliefs can create in us a wrong mindset which denies that God will raise us up and use us in this day.

## Consider

- How did Paul overcome adversity?
- How did Stephen impact Paul?
- Do you allow trouble to tell you a message about your worth?

# Thirteen

# *Confronting Confusion in Adversity*

*"But it won't be long before the weather clears
and the sun shines bright.
We'll see it all then,
see it all as clearly as God sees it,
knowing him directly just as he knows us!"*[29]

*The peace of God will soon*
*crush satan under your feet.*
(Romans 16:20 NIV)


*Trouble is a state of being distressed,*
*annoyed, upset,*
*afflicted or* **confused**.[30]


*T*he torrential rain had fallen relentlessly for the past two days
and now the storm was raging outside. With winds of up to
150 knots Cyclone Namu severely damaged much of the Solomon
Islands within a short 24 hours. It was after seven o'clock at night
when our baby Elisabeth awoke to water gushing in on her as it
torpedoed through the louvre windows. Moments later the force of
the wind ripped the roof off our back room. I had every reason to
imagine the worst. A powerful cyclone was threatening to lift our
house off its stilts and send it plummeting into the sea only metres
away.

Trying to get a grip on the situation, I remembered Psalm
46:1-3 which assured me that, even though the mountains should
fall into the sea, God would protect me and my family. This verse
gave me the peace I needed to survive the storm. I imagined God
himself surrounding our house.

Jill slept through the whole ordeal but Graham, older and
aware, lay terrified in his bed. Once Elisabeth was attended to, I
held Graham in my arms and prayed that Jesus would calm the
storm raging in his heart. As I prayed I became aware that God was
actually infusing an amazing peace into him. This peace enveloped
him like a thick wall of protection.

We have an identity as those who are able to walk in peace.
Just as an inheritance provides for the loved ones left after a relative
has died, so God has arranged an inheritance that provides twenty
four hour protection during life's storms. In a beautiful discourse

with the Father in John 17, Jesus 'writes' his will and leaves for us an inheritance of peace. *"Peace I leave with you, My peace I give to you"* (John 14:27 NIV). Our inheritance is a gift and a bona fide reflection of God's image. It cannot be earned; we are entitled to it because we are his children. Royalty are born into a realm of protection. Jesus, the prince of peace, invites us to live in his royal kingdom of unlimited peace. Imagine your worst case scenario and having peace greater than that! God, who is our peace, is greater than all the storms we face. *"But mightier than violent raging of the seas, mightier than the breakers on the shore - the Lord above is mightier than these* (Psalm 93: 4 NLT).

Our inheritance of peace is an important aspect in restoring our true value. It gives us unlimited resources to defeat fear. Embracing our inheritance ensures that we are protected from toxic thoughts that breed terror and dread in our hearts. God has intended that we enjoy abundant peace whilst living in a world gripped by fear. Yes, without a doubt the world is gripped by fear and insists that we are in danger. The risk of tsunamis, terrorism, cyclones and earthquakes intimidate us into believing the forces of nature and evil are greater than God.

> *Peace is a bona fide reflection of the very image of God.*

## God laughs

God sits in the heavens and laughs when the nations rage against him (Psalm 2:4). When storms rage against us do we laugh (Job 5:22) or are we overwhelmed? Are we outgoing and confident when storms lash our world, or do we cringe in fear? Mind you, it is very normal to be fearful when storms threaten our lives. Fear has its origins in spiritual darkness and ultimately exposes the unbelief in our hearts. Fear can overcome us to the point where we are consumed. If Jesus doesn't destroy our fears they will affect the way we think and respond to life.

## Confused

To walk in peace, we need to know who we really are. *"The days of the **blameless** are known to the Lord and their inheritance will endure for ever. In times of disaster they will not wither; in days of famine they will enjoy plenty"* (Psalm 37:18 NIV). Do we see ourselves as those who are blameless?

> *Masks cannot hide our shame forever and will eventually expose our pain.*

God gives our identity to us in seed form. It is imperishable. Depending on whether or not we water it with faith will determine whether it grows and becomes real in our lives. The more we believe that we are righteous, the more it will be able to form in us a strong identity. Knowing that we are righteous gives us everything needed to endure the journey.

Do you believe that your inheritance will last forever? We live in a day where nothing lasts forever. Relationships fail, clothes wear out, bodies age. God assures us that our inheritance will last forever. Having a lifelong inheritance enables us to remain peaceful in the presence of evil.

In the hope of destroying our inheritance of peace, the enemy uses trouble to confuse us. He spins us into emotional turmoil by convincing us that we aren't that righteous. To experience peace we need to believe that, although God may use trouble to test and discipline, he does not send trouble to punish us.

Consider Job, who felt that he was being punished. If we follow the conversations that he had with his friends and God, we will discover that Job was confused. Job knew in his head that he was righteous, but in his heart, he felt condemned. When his friends tried to confront his guilt he challenges their view and states that he is innocent. He says, *"Stop assuming my guilt, for I am righteous."*

Then to God, Job is honest and speaks frankly from his heart. *"If I have sinned, what have I done to you, O watcher of men? Why have you made me your target? Have I become a burden to you? Why do you not pardon my offences and forgive my sins?* (*Job 7:20-21 NIV*).

How often do we feel that God is punishing us when we experience the winds of adversity? If we forget who we are, free men and women rescued from death, the enemy will set up an internal war within our minds to sabotage God's peace.

Adversity has power to scribble disturbing messages deep within our hearts that we often cannot explain in words, but only feel. We consider ourselves invincible when life is free of problems. Health, status and affluence speak to us signifying our worth. Circumstances can easily change from that of peace and serenity to unexpected turbulence. When we lose the very things that give us worth we often feel the turbulence. How strong do we feel if we are suffering a chronic illness, or our job is taken from us or we have no money?

I have a friend who has constantly faced problems. Her large inheritance was stolen. Her family of origin disowned her, she suffered various forms of abuse earlier in her life and her daughter has been sick for many years. Recently she lost her job through an injustice, and now she is suffering many medical problems. After encouraging her to look to God, the Lord gently spoke to me and said, "Your friend thinks she deserves this treatment. She believes she is bad. Every time something goes wrong the enemy etches this view deeper into her heart." My friend has a strong faith in God, and enjoys a close relationship with him. She knows she is acceptable and righteous before him. But in her heart where she processes her feelings, there is something all together different going on.

During times of personal trouble, my distress has been increased by hidden fears regarding my identity. Unloved, unworthy, rejected and abandoned are just some of the many ways I have felt when I have faced trouble. When I have failed to embrace God's opinion of me I have opened myself up to be severely attacked.

I am not alone in this dilemma. God used trouble to draw attention to Jobs' damaged image. *"Your real motive, your true intent, was to watch me, and if I sinned, you would not forgive my guilt"* (Job 10:13 NLT). You see, Job's knowledge of God was based on the flawed assumption that God was harsh. His situation worsened because he neither understood the nature of God (God is kind) nor his own standing before him as righteous.

## A place of safety

When passing through turbulent times and our self-image is attacked it is vital that we find a place of protection. Psalm 91 offers us such a place. *"Surely he will save you from the fowler's snare and from the deadly pestilence. He will cover you with his feathers and under his wings you will find refuge"* (Psalm 91:4 NIV).

The Greek word for *cherish* is *thalpo* and conveys the idea of "birds covering their young with their feathers."[31] When battling the storms of life it is vital that we feel cherished by God. Being cherished makes us feel loved and thereby empower us to understand that we are not being punished.

In troubling times God desires that we run to him so that he can gather us up in his arms and protect us with his reassuring presence. Our place of safety is found in his name. *"The name of the Lord is a strong tower; the righteous run to it and are safe"*

(Proverbs 18:10 NIV).

## *Fragile masks*

If we fail to run into God's arms and find his comfort, we may then hide our pain behind masks. From a very early age we learn to use masks to protect ourselves from the harsh messages we receive. These masks hide our painful response to trouble. Food, shallow relationships and alcohol are some of the masks we can hide behind when we experience adversity. Such coping mechanisms prevent us from acknowledging the full depth of pain felt in our hearts. Food and drink were never designed to anesthetise emotional pain. Many of us fail to understand that such masks are damaging; they become more obviously transparent and fragile later in life. As a nurse, I have seen many illnesses resulting from alcohol. Whilst training I nursed an alcoholic who had become a paraplegic through his inability to stop his drinking addiction.

> *Trouble has the power to confuse us.*

Masks cannot hide our shame and will eventually expose our pain. Many of us know this and have an inner desire to abandon such masks. This desire is seen in recent movies such as *I am Sam* and *Wit*. Rita Harrison in *I am Sam* hid her shame of being disposable behind the life of a successful lawyer. Vivian Bearing in the film *Wit* hid behind the mask of philosophy before a terminal illness exposed her distorted image and revealed the frightened little girl that she had always been.

## *Are you facing a storm?*

We often feel a sense of powerlessness when facing the storms of life. When the enemy stripped the land, Gideon was so confused

109

that he fled and hid in the winepress. Gideon hid his sense of powerlessness behind a mask of "work." God destroyed all Gideon's fear by revealing to him the place where he could find his true strength and protection. *"The Lord is with you, mighty warrior"* (Judges 6: 11 NIV). Gideon discovered that God was in fact bigger than his enemy. No longer could the impending situation overpower him.

> *Rays flashed from his hand,*
> *where his power was hidden.*
> (Habakkuk 3: 4 NIV)

God's power is hidden in his hand; it is with his right hand that God holds us. *"Do not fear, for I am with you; do not be dismayed for I am your God. I will strength you and help you; I will uphold you with my righteous right hand* (Isaiah 41:10 NIV). That same power by which God upholds the universe is the same power that upheld Gideon and made him a mighty warrior.

*Death is any place where God is not present.*

God showed Gideon that he was protected. Then he did something really amazing. He spoke into the hidden lie that was feeding Gideon's fear. Fear of death has the power to throw us into confusion. We are all born with a fear of death and trouble magnifies this fear. Whether it is loss of life, relationships or livelihood we all fear losing the very thing that has become part of our life. Death is any place where God is not present. God speaks into this fear with the truth. *"Peace do not be afraid, you are not going to die."* To recapture the moment, *"Gideon built an altar to the Lord there and called it The Lord is Peace"* (Judges 6:23-24 NIV).

The outcome of having a good understanding of our worth is an increased level of peace. The Greek word for *peace* is *sigao* and means to be silent.[32] God desires that we weather our storms devoid of all inner conflict. He doesn't want us to imagine the worst. We can live in a realm of peace and remain silent even during the worst of life's storms.

## Consider

What do these verses tell you about your current situation?

- Revelation 21:7
- 1 Corinthians 1:8
- Colossians 2:10
- 2 Corinthians 1:21
- Romans 8:37
- 2 Corinthians 2:14-15

*And the God of all grace,*
*who called you to his eternal*
*glory in Christ, after you*
*have suffered a little while,*
*will himself restore you will*
*make you strong, firm and steadfast.*
(1 Peter 5:10 NIV)

# Fourteen

# The Miracle

*Wake up, wake up*
*flex your muscles, God!* [33]

*T*he day was sunny and the seas were calm but suddenly, without warning, a gale force wind arose. Never before had the waves become so great that they prevented us from reaching our destination. We sheltered overnight in a lagoon. Needless to say I was determined to get off the boat the following morning and get a truck back to Auki and, from there travel between islands on a larger boat. Brian was not afraid and told me that we would stay on the boat. I was petrified and this fear needed to be dealt with. There, while anchored in the safe haven of the lagoon, I went into our cabin and told God all about the looming danger. Instead of pretending to be brave, I blurted out my terror and concern for my precious son and daughters. It was then that God guaranteed me that we would have "a smooth passage".

The following morning, after unloading cargo at a village further up the coast, we began the long journey across to Honiara. Just as the shoreline disappeared from sight the captain came down from his cabin and told us that the instruments were indicating that danger was imminent. I thought: "Oh no, we are going to drown!" How I wished we were safely back on land.

But then I remembered God's promise. Recognising that this was my cue to make a difference, I made my way out of the cabin onto the deck and, sitting down, I asked Jesus to show me his power over the wind and the waves. I realised that even before I spoke, God had already planned to flex his muscles and reveal his power. Believing that God would act enabled me to speak to the storm and say, "Be still". Before my very eyes, the winds calmed down and the seas became like a millpond. It all happened so quickly. I walked over to the edge of the boat and saw my face mirrored in the glassy water. We were astonished, so much so that no one said a word. Everyone sat reflective, as if miles away. It was not until many years later that I could actually talk about this openly. I could write home about it, but I couldn't talk, such was the presence of God at that moment.

Our storms in life can affect the way we see ourselves. They can make us doubt our worth and make us feel that God is against us. The storms that we experience are not always physical. We don't have to experience a gale force wind to feel the effects that pressure can have on our lives. A storm can be an inner turmoil or deep conflict caused by depression and paranoia. Bankruptcy or the loss of a job can cause despair and threaten our significance. Loss of relationship with family and friends can threaten our sense of belonging.

> *When we focus on God, the size of our problems diminishes*

## *Don't focus on your storm*

Many times we try to still storms by focusing on them. Often we think that if we can just concentrate hard enough, our problems will resolve. We can't overcome our challenges if we are looking at their size. The secret to overcoming our challenge is to get our eyes off their size and fix our gaze on God.

Shadrach, Meshach and Abenigo's dilemma began with a deliberate refusal to bow down to an image of gold that king Nebuchadnezzar had set up. As a result the king was offended and they were *"bound and thrown into the blazing furnace"* (Daniel 3:21 NIV). Whilst in the furnace they re-directed their eyes from the flames and focused them on God. As they walked about unbound and unharmed, a fourth person walked with them (Daniel 3: 16-25). Their focus enabled them to see God in the midst of great trials. They survived a fiery furnace.

But suppose our fiery furnace is a challenge from which we feel there is no escape. Perhaps we have become physically disabled or suffering a chronic disease; we may be living in a war torn country or have become locked into a relationship that appears to be without hope. When feeling trapped, by looking away from our situation and focusing on God, we are given a way of escape.

As a young seventeen year old, Joni Erickson had everything at her feet. She was tall and beautiful; life was promising. One fateful day, this all changed when she dived into a shallow pool, breaking her spine, becoming a quadriplegic. Desperate and wanting to end her days, she cried out to God and discovered a power that gave her a determination to make something beautiful from the pieces of her broken life. God reinterpreted her circumstance with the truth. He became her light, enabling her to see her significance and value in the midst of great tragedy.

> *Faith enables us to face the impossible.*

Often we think that the weaker we are, the more powerful our problems will become. The opposite is true. It is our weakness, not our strength, that gives God the perfect opportunity to help us. How can God help us if we don't need him? I plan to always need God; for it is when we need him, in the place of our inadequacy, that we can see his power.

When we focus on God, the size of our problem diminishes. *"The chariots of God are tens of thousands and thousands and thousands"* (Psalm 68:17 NIV). Compared to God, the nations sit as dust on the scales of the universe. The waters are held in the palm of his hand (Psalm 40). In the known cosmos there are three hundred and fifty billion galaxies. In our galaxy, the Milky Way, there are two hundred billion stars. Yet, God made all of this and his own size is unfathomable. Focusing on God puts our problems into their proper perspective.

# Power of imagination

*Faith is the confidence that what we hope for will actually happen;*
*it gives us the assurance about things we cannot see* (Hebrews 11:1
NLT). Do you believe that what you hope for will actually happen?
Some imagine living on a yacht and believe it will happen. When
we place our faith in faith we place our faith in the object of our
desire. Having faith in faith assumes that we can receive anything
for which we have faith.

Faith in God is different from faith in faith. When we
have faith in God, rather than the object, we place our faith in the
One who can supply our desire. If we don't believe that God is a
lavishing, generous God, we will not be able to believe him for
the impossible. If I had not believed that God had plans to bless us
and not to harm us, I may have only allowed the promise that we
would have a safe journey to penetrate my mind. However, because
I believed God and trusted his character, his promise penetrated the
inner place of my imagination. I actually saw the millpond water.

Faith believes that what we hope for will actually happen.
It has total confidence in God's goodness. Faith makes us men
and women of exceptional strength. Faith enables us to face the
impossible.

We often read the Word with our mind. Our mind is part
of the carnal nature and continually wars against the things of the
Spirit (Romans 7:14-20). The imagination is part of the heart with
which we see. We rarely forget what we see. Our imagination is
a powerful tool in the hand of God and, when used properly, can
translate God's thoughts into our heart. If we can see the truth in
our imagination it will become real. If we believe that we have
been raised with Christ then we should be able to see ourselves
sitting in the heavenly places far about all our problems.

Allowing the Word to penetrate our imagination creates a
joy that can't be taken from us. *"The joy of the Lord is our strength"*

*(Nehemiah 8:10 NIV).* I remember the joy I felt when I decided to challenge the gale force winds. With the promise of God in my hand I felt invincible. Such strength gave me inbuilt buoyancy that enabled me to leap over that particular obstacle I was facing.

Having insight into God's greatness and goodness will lift us above our circumstances. As we focus on God, we become caught up in his loveliness. The sheer joy of his presence distracts us from our dilemmas. When our imagination is filled with the image of God we will be transformed into his likeness.

At the beginning of each trial, remember who you are. Put on the belt of truth; see yourself as a strong courageous overcomer. See your enemy under your feet. With that vision, face your trial ... and watch it bow to you.

Everything, and that means everything, that we go through works together for our good (Romans 8:28). Our trials give God the perfect opportunity to reveal his love and power. Knowing that we are protected by God prevents a defeatist attitude destroying our lives. If we remain calm and stand firm in the situation, a strength, which may only be evident in months to come, will be developed within us.

We all can bounce back when the enemy knocks us down. Is your attitude becoming more confident? Are you going higher and moving forward or are you standing still because of the trouble you are facing? Are you stepping over your problems or are you falling under their weight?

> *The salvation of the righteous comes*
> *from the Lord; he is their stronghold in*
> *times of trouble. The Lord helps them*
> *and delivers them; he delivers them from*
> *the wicked and saves them, because*
> *they take refuge in him.* (Psalm 37:39 NIV)

Refuges are set up to protect vulnerable people from danger and the elements. God himself becomes our refuge and fortress. Imagine yourself under the shadow of God's wing. Imagine him surrounding you, protecting you as a fortress would protect a besieged city. As you allow God's Word to penetrate your imagination you will emerge from trouble with a clearer perception of yourself.

Gaining our protection from God enables us to become spiritually strong. The word *strong* carries with it the idea of "having the power of resistance: able to withstand great force or opposition; not easily damaged or overcome."[34] Being able to endure trials enables us to develop an excellent spirit. Rather than losing our cool or becoming depressed during challenging times we can rise up and show to the world our true colours.

God is profoundly positive, always taking us to a place where we can look beyond our circumstances. He is incredibly faithful in developing our understanding of our true identity and deeply loyal to the vision he has of us. Every time we are honest about how we feel God will rub more tarnish off our old image. He will reveal to us more of our true beauty. In times of testing God changes our view of ourselves and mirrors back to us an image that gives courage to soar above the storms of life.

## Consider

- Are there people and situations too big for you to handle?
- Are we gaining God's perspective so that we can become strong?
- Are you placing your faith in God or are you placing your faith in your desired object?

*Without faith it is impossible to please*
*God because anyone who comes to him*
*must first believe that he exists*
*and that he rewards*
*those who earnestly*
*seek him.*

(Hebrews 11:6 NIV)

# Fifteen

# Pleasing God

*But when the Son of Man returns, how many will he find on the earth who have faith?*
*(Luke 18:8 NLT)*

*D*o you have faith to believe for a miracle? Many years ago our church showed some video footage of a powerful spiritual wind force that touched thousands sitting in a packed overseas stadium. I will neither forget the noise nor the resulting impact of that wind. Many in the stadium were healed and profoundly affected by the supernatural power of God.

In a prayer meeting months later our family friend Josh asked me to pray for his paperwork that had been piling up on his desk. God gave me a picture of the *Wind of God* helping him get twice as much work done in half the time. As I began to pray, God released his supernatural power. Josh recalls the wind force that went through him actually caused his shirt to cling to his body. This wind force was so powerful that as it went through Josh, it knocked over the person standing behind him. We are not here just to get up every morning to have breakfast, read our Bibles (or the paper), go to work, come home, watch television, shower, and go to bed; only to wake up the next day to repeat the whole routine again. We are placed on this planet to live in awesome wonder. We are designed to experience divine encounters every moment of every day. But for this to happen we need to see ourselves the way God sees us. When we live according to how God sees us we will be able to partner with heaven and touch earth.

Many times I have stood in wonder at God's miracle-working power. While in the Solomon Islands, I met a young couple who were looking for the ideal lifestyle. I had come over to the capital, Honiara, from our home at Onepusu to have some dental work done. That night Mark and Leanne happened to sit down at the dinner table, at the transit house, at the same time as I did. This was my first time meeting this lovely couple and we quickly became engaged in a conversation centering on why I was in the Solomons. Mark, being of Jewish heritage, became incensed that I was sharing my faith with the indigenous people. I had never met anyone quite like Mark. In all his accusations and arguing, I saw a heart that was searching, so I was patient with him. After much debate Mark stunned me with his desire to come back to Onepusu with the view of finding out more about Jesus. Once at Onepusu I used every theological argument possible but nothing worked. I felt so frustrated that such debating lacked power.

A couple of nights later the moon's soft light shone on the empty fishing net as Brian dragged it ashore. It is important to note two things here: there was a full moon and secondly fish have both eyes and brains. They can see the net if the moon is full and they are clever enough to dodge it. As the net lay limp on the beach I had a vision of it filled with fish. Without thinking I heard myself saying to my Jewish friend, "To prove that Jesus is alive I am going to ask him to fill that net with fish tomorrow night." I knew I was asking God for the impossible but I was confident because I had already seen it in a vision. The next night the net was full. My friend believed in Jesus.

> *We don't realise how much we live in unbelief until we are confronted with a miracle that we cannot explain.*

## Dangerous wonder

The opening of blind eyes and deaf ears, the strengthening of legs and the curing of diseases could not be explained by the natural mind. As Jesus held a constant gaze toward the Father, his body became a divine conduit connecting heaven to earth. Likewise we can become a conduit when we connect our faith to the energy surge of the *dynamis* power of God.

*Incomparable great power for us who believe. That power is like the working of His mighty strength, which He exerted in Christ when He raised Him from the dead and seated Him at His right hand in the heavenly realms.*
(Ephesians 1:19-20 NIV)

Are you armed with faith? Do you live on the edge of expectancy? Have you become dangerous to the demonic realm? God desires that we be aware of situations that can reveal his power; he desires that we partner with heaven so that he can touch earth with his glory.

> *When we live according to how God sees us we will be able to partner with heaven and touch earth.*

Miracles are intended to reveal God's character and a person's worth. In bringing heaven to earth, Jesus placed underserved value on every person that he came into contact with. He lifted the dignity of man by referring to some as his own children. The woman who reached out and touched his garment, he affectionately called daughter. *"Take heart, daughter,"* he said, *"your faith has healed you"* (Matthew 9:20-22 NIV).

The woman at the well discovered her value through a simple conversation with the "living water" (John 4:1-26). On the Day of Pentecost, God's glory penetrated the atmosphere in the upper room and within a short time infiltrated the market place. God's glory is designed for everyday living. It is to be experienced at work, in our homes and among friendships.

A dilemma arises because we live in a world where our minds are focused on the physical realm, not the spiritual. In our western world common sense tells us that wind does not heal people nor does it change their lives. Common sense erroneously tells us that our rational arguments have more power to incite faith than a net full of fish.

## Logic excludes faith

Peter threw all logic aside and completely forgot about drowning when he leapt out of the boat into wild seas. But when Peter took his eyes off Jesus, he realised where he was, and logic kicked back in and he started to sink (Matthew 14:29-31). We tend to have faith in what we understand in our minds. To our natural mind water is not a platform on which to walk. In the natural realm, for reasons of safety and practicality, we need common sense. But in the supernatural realm, we must put our logical thinking aside and trust in a God who acts outside of the laws of logic.

We don't realise how much we live in unbelief until we are confronted with a miracle that we cannot explain. Jesus came face to face with unbelief when he delivered a mute boy from an evil spirit. The crowds were impressed but the Pharisees *"were left sputtering, 'Hocus pocus. It's nothing but hoscus pocus. He's probably made a pact with the Devil '"*[35]. Linking the spiritual world to our physical world is our biggest challenge. We often fail to link these two worlds because we are hesitant to trust ourselves to a God who cannot be tamed by logic.

Royree Jensen, in her book *Naked Unbelief*, states that as "we have a mindset that exalts logic, science, philosophies, outward beauty and education; it should come as no surprise that Christians in the western world only try to argue the gospel logically, with a conspicuous absence of the power of God."[36] In this age of reason, we have faith in what we can see. We have this idea that we have become infallible because we have conquered so much. There is so much that is no longer a mystery to us. Space no longer seems unfathomable and medical science has almost ventured into the sacred whereby humans are able to be cloned. We need to have the humility to surrender our lives, give up our pride and realise that there are limits to our powers of reason. We must come to a place of childlike acceptance where we no longer try to work everything out.

> *Without faith it is impossible to please*
> *God because anyone who comes to him*
> *must first believe that he exists*
> *and that he rewards those who earnestly seek him.*
> (Hebrews 11:6 NIV)

## *What is faith?*

Because we have grown up thinking and behaving according to our cultural ways we need a paradigm shift in the way we think. If we don't believe that are made to become like God, it is unlikely that we will. Do you want exceptional strength of character? Then work on getting a picture of how God sees you into your imagination. God is extravagant, he lavishes his love and gifts on us. He desires that we become like him even more than we do. When we have intimate knowledge of how God sees us we too will confront natural common sense. Being men and women of faith we are not to listen to any voice that tells us we have little worth. We are supernatural beings and by increasing our awareness of God we are more able to see our true likeness. God desires to release faith to our spirit so that we can accept that we are who he says we are. Having God re-define our identity is one of the greatest miracles that he can perform.

If we don't have faith it will be impossible to please God. As part of our armour we have been given a shield to extinguish all the fiery darts of the enemy. To use the shield of faith we need to become as little children. Children have implicit trust; they accept without question what they are told. We need to become as children so that we can believe that we are made to reflect God *"Abraham believed the Lord and he credited it to him as righteousness"* (Genesis 15: 6 NIV). Abraham became as a child and walked in simple faith as he placed his audacious confidence in God and as a result he was declared righteous (Genesis 15:6).

*"As the body without the spirit is dead, so faith without deeds is dead"* (James 2:26 NIV). To be effective, our faith has to be expressed in our actions. We cannot believe that we are made in God's image and live in such a way that negates that belief. If we fail to act on our faith, we enter into confusion and will not experience transformation. The Bible tells of people who lived with the knowledge of their true identity. These people would never have been able to display God's power and glory had they used logical reasoning. In giving her last penny to God the widow defied logic (Luke 21:2). The Israelites marched around Jericho for seven days. Then at the sound of the trumpet blast and a shout from the people, the walls fell defying natural common sense (Joshua 6:5). Paul's message that we are saved by grace challenges logical thinking (Romans 4:5).

> *Having God redefine our identity is one of the greatest miracles that he can perform.*

> *And what more shall I say? I do not have time to tell about Gideon, Barak, Samson, Jephthah, David, Samuel and the prophets, who through faith conquered kingdoms, administered justice, and gained what was promised; who shut the mouths of lions, quenched the fury of the flames, and escaped the edge of the sword; whose weakness was turned to strength; and who become powerful in battle and routed foreign armies.* (Hebrews 11:32-38 NIV)

# Winners

Acting on their faith in God made these people winners. Rain, hail or shine these great men and women of faith knew who they were. They were unstoppable. They had outright determination and were relentless in their belief that they were who God said they were: invincible, unbeatable, conquering "image reflectors". The faith within these people mirrored an image of heaven. We also are designed to reveal the eternal realm of heaven. We cannot reflect anything that we are not looking at. 2 Corinthians 4:18 says, "*Now we fix our eyes on not what is seen but what is unseen. For what is seen is temporal, but what is unseen is eternal.*" We fix our eyes on the unseen by believing God. Our faith in God is very powerful; it ought not to be wasted believing philosophies that do not reveal God's character. It is as we live out our God given identity that we will be able to partner with heaven and touch earth. To believe God is to activate our faith. As we agree with God concerning our identity we come into harmony with the most powerful force in the universe.

## Consider

- Is your faith aggressive?
- Do you seek to push back the obstacles that prevent God's glory from being seen?
- What does it mean that "faith without works is dead?"

# *Sixteen*

# *The Test*

*Consider it pure joy, my brothers,
whenever you face trials of many kinds,
because you know the testing of your faith
develops perseverance.*
(James 1:2-3 NIV)

*But the meek (in the end)
shall inherit the earth,
and shall delight themselves
in the abundance of peace.* [37]

*L*et's recap. The enemy and his cohorts are very aware of our ability to destroy their network of darkness. They plan to strip power from us and ultimately render us ineffective. Using negative words and difficult circumstances the enemy causes us to doubt our worth. If we believe that we don't matter then it becomes easy to ignore what God says about us. An excerpt from Nelson Mandela's inaugural speech reflects this thought.

> Our deepest fear is
> not that we are inadequate.
> Our deepest fear is
> that we are powerful beyond measure.
> It is our light, not our darkness.
> that most frightens us.[38]

The idea of being God's counterpart has become so far removed from our sense of identity that it seems mystic, unreal and downright imaginary. Rarely do we understand the significance the supernatural has in helping us to find ourselves. My guess is that if we did understand we wouldn't fear the light of God within.

We have received the fullness of Christ. We are made to be a reflector of his great power. Nothing can separate us from God's love. These amazing truths define who we are. God often tests us to see how well we have understood these truths.

*If you fall to pieces in a crisis, there wasn't much to you in the first place* [39]

Failing a test is a painful experience. No one likes to fail. Failing our tests means that we *fall to pieces* in a crisis. But God is so gracious, he allows us to re- sit our tests as many times as needed.

## How to fail the test

Often my tests have involved painful and complex relationships where I have become offended, rejected and misunderstood. Because I have become caught up in the complexity of these situations, I have become frightened and confused, and mostly have ended up feeling sorry for myself.

We will fail if the opinion of man is more important to us than the opinion of God and if the physical world is more urgent than the spiritual. We will fail particularly if we define ourselves by our circumstances and if we fail to have a vision of how God sees us.

## Clues to passing the test

The test is an open book exam and we are expected to ask God for the answers. One of the requirements necessary for passing the test is that we apply what we are told and put into practice what we see and hear in the Word.

To pass the test we have to know it is a test. If we don't know that our difficult situations are testing our character, we might fail to ask God for the answers. Knowing that we are being tested enables us to search for the answers while enduring our trial.

To pass our tests we need to remember who we are. Let's remind ourselves of our identity as God sees us. We are:

- counterpart of God
- pinnacle of creation
- chosen to be like him
- light in a dark place
- righteous
- beautiful
- majestic

You would think that in having these images in our imagination we would enjoy a test occasionally and possibly even anticipate being tested. But because we forget who we are, we see tests as intruders and rarely do we welcome them as friends.

God desires that we anticipate his tests. He checks to see how deeply our true identity has penetrated into our hearts. Has the vision of being loved and righteous become superficial, lying on the edge of our minds, or has it been planted deep in the good soil of our hearts where it can grow? If we haven't got a picture of how God sees us firmly placed in our imagination, it will then be easily forgotten in the trials of life.

Passing the test involves finding the truth about who we really are and then using that truth to fight off negative imagery. Because the enemy fights with imagery based on lies, we must counter attack with imagery based on truth.

God has clearly told us that we are strong, but the enemy paints an image of weakness in our mind. To destroy images of weakness, search in the book of Nehemiah, Daniel and Revelations for images of the strength that God has given you. Fight negative image with positive image. Don't put up with weak pictures of yourself. Place in your mind imagery that sends the enemy running. See yourself moving boulders and speaking to mountains. See the enemy cringing before you

If the devil tells you that you are evil, then journey with God into the book of Romans until you find the impeccable righteousness that God has placed within you. We are to use the image of being righteous to destroy the lie that we are evil.

If you feel abandoned, seek verses from the book of Psalms and Isaiah until you understand that your true sense of belonging cannot be taken from you. Remember to use what you learn during your battles.

The enemy says that we are ugly. To destroy this lie use the truth that we are beautiful. Use pictures from the Song of Songs;

weaken the enemy's image by using the Word as your weapon. If the enemy has smeared an image of being ugly over your life, it is only because he is afraid of the beauty within you. If he has told you that you are insignificant, then he is only trying to prevent you discovering your destiny in becoming part of God's dream team. The key to unlocking our identity is found in finding the lie controlling our life and then exchanging that lie for the truth. For every lie the enemy has planted, God has a truth that will powerfully destroy that lie.

> *Knowing we are loved unconditionally empowers us to live confidently.*

## The test of meekness

Fighting negative imagery with positive imagery enables us to become meek. Jesus has given us a book of imagery that enables us to become like him. He at all times was meek. One of the most forgotten beatitudes is meekness. With the loud and pushy people gaining all the attention and a 'right to fight' attitude so prevalent today, it appears we have lost the true art of being meek. Many of us hold an erroneous concept of what it means to be meek. We don't usually associate meek people with those who are confident and assertive. Instead, we associate meekness with those who are spineless; those who mumble under their breath, and with the unnoticed and introverted. The dictionary's definition of meekness supports this imagery and implies that a meek person is "weak, timid, docile, spiritless mild bland and wimpish".[40] The damage to this word is perhaps outrageously irreparable. No one likes to appear weak and helpless, even less so bland and spiritless.

Timid people are nervous and apprehensive and are impotent to rise up and face their trials in power and strength. Meekness is not weak. The apprehensive will never inherit anything, let alone the earth. Nowhere in the Scripture does God expect us to be timid nor does he leave us exposed or vulnerable to our circumstances. In fact, it is clearly stated in the Scriptures that, *"God has not given us a spirit of fear and timidity, but of power, love and self-discipline"* (2 Timothy 1:7 NKJV).

God desires that we become strong men and women, who are confident in our worth. He desires that we are able to rise up and overcome our challenges. *"From the days of John the Baptist until now, the kingdom of heaven has been forcefully advancing, and forceful men lay hold of it"* (Matthew 11:12 NIV). We are reminded *"that the righteous are bold as a lion"* (Proverbs 28:1 NIV). Discovering our true identity empowers us to be transformed from a kitten into a bold lion.

Brenda walked in meekness when she allowed God's word to penetrate her imagination during a severe medical challenge that affected her husband, Adrian. When I first saw Adrian he was in the Intensive Care Unit on a ventilator. He had fallen unconscious after an operation to remove a bowel blockage and, medically the situation looked to be an impossible challenge. As I walked to Adrian's bedside God spoke and said that he was going to "raise Adrian up out of a bed of sickness into total health."

Brenda allowed this word to sink into her troubled mind and amazingly took hold of the sword of the Spirit and began to fight. Brenda is a prayer warrior. She has fought for people in the past and seen many great victories. But she was yet to find out just how invincible God had made her to be.

Adrian contracted a hospital infection which damaged the valve in his heart. As a result he had to have open heart surgery. He had many complications; fighting oedema, a collapsed lung and kidney failure. What started out as a quick visit to the hospital to rectify a small problem lasted five months. With every new challenge, the warrior in Brenda rose up in prayer and destroyed everything that threatened Adrian's health. Throughout Adrian's stay in hospital I saw a profound gentleness and patience in Brenda. She didn't become fearful when Adrian nearly died but was calm and confident.

Being a meek person, Brenda knew she didn't have to prove anything in the face of her adversity. On one of my visits to pray with her, Brenda said, "Jenny, I am coming to realise just how big God is. I am feeling like nothing has the power to destroy Adrian's future." Brenda connected who she was, with who God is. This connection enabled her to rise up in boldness and confidence. Because Brenda depended on having the right connections, she saw God's power work on her behalf. She chose neither to be intimidated, nor overwhelmed, but took out the Word of God, and using that as her weapon, destroyed the works of the enemy that were targeting her precious husband. Today Adrian is enjoying life to the full.

> *One of the most forgotten beatitudes is meekness*

Let's get it straight here. We are not designed to be timid when going through tough times. Meek people are fully aware of the vision God has of them. Knowing who they are shields them from having to prove themselves when walking through adversity. We can confidently pass our tests when we know that the waters of trouble won't be overwhelming (Isaiah 43:2). Those who pass the test of trouble know that when the challenges of life are becoming too hot, and the flames of affliction are dancing at their feet, they will not be burnt.

## *Meekness before God makes us great in his eyes*

Self-control is the key to becoming meek. We all want to pass our tests but are we prepared to be delivered from the enemy of self-will and impatience? We can't become meek if we fly off the handle and erupt at a moment's notice. Nor can we be meek if we see ourselves as small. To be meek we need to see ourselves as those who are loved, righteous, strong and beautiful; designed to receive God's goodness. Knowing our worth enables us to respond quietly and confidently, rather than reacting harshly during our trials.

> *When our identity is bigger than our challenges, adversity will not intimidate us.*

Moses finally came to understand his true worth. So much so that he became the meekest man on earth. By gaining his identity from God, he passed his tests. However he wasn't always meek. He grew up in a palace as a prince of Egypt. The constant attention he received shaped him into a man of natural strength and arrogance. He might even have been labelled pushy when he got involved in a fight that wasn't his. In fear, he fled to the wilderness. It was there that God intercepted him and gave him a new frame of reference to rebuild his character. This new frame of reference was God himself. Moses became an unpretentious and patient man.

## The meek are not afraid

Meek people are gentle and patient because they are not afraid. They carry such a strong sense of identity that they do not have to prove themselves. Joseph passed all his tests and eventually became Prime Minister of Egypt. Even when he was rejected by his brothers, he walked with unusual self-assurance. He held a confident composure when he was hurled into a pit, sold into slavery and locked behind prison bars. He remained focused, even when for many years his situation worsened. Nothing fazed him. Why? Joseph knew who he was. Embracing his worth gave him amazing courage. He didn't make regrettable decisions but instead always knew what to do. Knowing he was favoured by his father gave him a great sense of value when the storms crashed over his life. He overcame every obstacle the enemy threw at him. In Genesis, we read an overview of this victory:

> *With bitterness archers attacked him; they shot at him with hostility, but his bow remained steady, his strong arm stayed limber, because of the hand of the Almighty One of Jacob, because of the shepherd, the rock of Israel, because of your father's God, who helps you, because of the Almighty who blesses you.*
> (Genesis 49:23-25 NIV)

## *Are you patient?*

Every challenge that we face can be overcome in the presence of God. It is while in his presence that he becomes our shield and protection. *"But the Lord is with me like a mighty warrior"* (Jeremiah 20:11 NIV). The bigger the problem we face, the clearer our picture needs to be of ourselves as those who are being held in the hand of an outstanding and amazingly powerful God.

If we don't know our true worth, we will fail our test by becoming impatient and defensive. Throughout the movie, *As it is in Heaven*, the characters exploded, unleashing a volcano of violent emotions. Because lies had formed their identities, suspicion within the group was rife, they were unable to be real with themselves and with each other. Daniel, who had a passion to see people realise their worth, intercepted their angry outbursts with amazing love and patience. He made each person, in their worst moment, feel accepted and valued. This in turn gave them the courage to become real.

Knowing we are loved unconditionally empowers us to live confidently. Nothing will confuse or frighten us. Devoid of fear, we will be certain that God is in control. *"In quietness and trust is your strength"* (Isaiah 30:15 NIV). Possessing such confidence gives us the courage to allow God to mould us into meek people who become "unassuming, patient, yielding."[41]

When everything is falling apart in our lives, God alone has the right to shape our image. But for this to happen we need to hear what God has to say. Jesus never pushes his way into our lives; he patiently waits to be invited into our problems so he can redefine our identity.

## How do you see yourself?

Have you allowed God to tell you who you really are? Has his opinion made you bold and confident when the waves of adversity have crashed over your life? Has your identity become mature and well-developed, not deficient in any way? Or have the challenges that you have faced become bigger than how you have seen yourself?

When our identity is bigger than our challenges, adversity will not intimidate us. When we see ourselves as overcomers we will become overcomers. This doesn't mean that life will be a breeze and that we won't be exposed to situations that cause suffering and pain. It does mean that these circumstances will not affect the way we see ourselves.

## Consider

- How do we fail our tests?
- How do we pass our tests?
- What does it mean to be meek?
- Why aren't meek people afraid?
- Do you run away at the sight of trouble or do you face your problem?

# Section Two

# *Seventeen*

# *Hiding Behind the Door of our Hearts*

*For out of the overflow of the heart the mouth speaks.*
(Matthew 12:34 NIV)

*W*hen we have been offended, intimidated or have suffered adversity our hearts can become so wounded that we no longer believe that God is good and that we are loved. The faith level in our hearts shift down a notch or two. Rather than having a soft responsive heart we build walls around our tender emotions that prevent us from reaching out to God.

> *"guard your heart above all else, for it determines the course of your life."*

If we hide our pain it will be easy to shut God out of our lives. Rather than believing that we are forgiven, we harbour self-hatred, feed our minds with negativity and do our own thing. Perhaps we read our Bibles but don't allow the Word of God to affect our thoughts. The outcome of this is that we no longer desire to please God but rather we spend our lives pleasing people. Can you detect a downward spiral happening here? The outcome is one that the enemy delights in. He wants to steal our faith so that we live in discouragement and despair.

In the Old Testament the priests had turned away from the living God. Although they still appeared to be worshipping God they were found to be worshipping idols behind the inner door of the temple. This "inner door" represents a place in our hearts that only God can see. Sometimes we cannot see what we are bowing down to in the inner places of our hearts. God has shaped our hearts and he alone knows what is in there. He cares deeply about the belief systems we are forming and the distance these are creating between him and us.

The temple in Jerusalem was desecrated and the priests could no longer go behind the "inner door" to worship God. Nehemiah, who understood the necessity of the temple, then rebuilt it and restored it to its original glory. The temple represents our hearts. Do you not know that your body is the temple of the Holy Spirit? (1 Corinthians 6:19-20) Your heart is the dwelling place of God. Into the temple of our hearts God has shone his light (2 Corinthians 4:6), poured out his love (Romans 5:5), and placed his Spirit (2 Corinthians 1:22). He has done this to prepare a place for Jesus to live (Ephesians 3:17).

God uses circumstances of life, both good and bad, to search our hearts and test them (Romans 8:27, 1 Thessalonians 2:4). He can do this because he has shaped our hearts. The very hearts that he has shaped have the capacity to turn away from him (Psalm 95:10). Even though we have set up idols in the inner places of our being, God has power to recapture our hearts (Ezekiel 14:5). He does this by refreshing and encouraging us. (Philemon verse 7, Colossians 14:8).

Our hearts will determine the direction that we take in life. Therefore it is vital that we prevent our hearts becoming allured by that which will ultimately destroy our desire to find our true selves. We are to protect and guard our hearts, *"guard your heart above all else, for it determines the course of your life."* (Proverbs 4:23 NLT)

## Consider

- What do these verses tell us about our hearts?
- 1 Thessalonians 2:4
- 1 Thessalonians 3:13
- 2 Thessalonians, 3:5 Philemon 7
- Hebrews 10:16
- Romans 8:27, Colossians 1 4:8

Destructive imagery
is
a hidden
but powerful weapon
the enemy uses
to
defame our identity.

# Eighteen

# Warped Mirrors

*For if we could control our tongues*
*we would be perfect*
*and could also have power over ourselves*
*in every way.*
(James 3:2 NLT)

*T*oday was fantastically glorious. The gentle autumn sun warmed my back as I sat overlooking the water enjoying morning tea with a friend. After lunch I finished reading a heart warming novel and enjoyed the remains of the afternoon working on the computer. A pretty good day, you might say? Yet at dinner tonight I felt uneasy, in fact edgy. Retracing my steps I realised that during the day I read an article that had made me feel ugly inside my heart. There was a time when I wasn't always diligent in paying attention to my reactions. I have realised over many years of ignoring my emotions, that what we ignore becomes buried and waits for the day when a trigger awakens it, and then we suddenly react.

A simple test as to whether or not we have a healthy view of our worth is found in observing our emotions. Our emotions are often a sign or symptom of deeper issues. In the medical world, a bruise is a sign, a headache is a symptom. One is seen, the other is felt, but both are indicators of deeper problems. Our negative emotions tell us that we have a problem and often become keys that help us unlock the lies buried in our hearts.

Do we want to be men and women full of faith and power? James asks that question this way. Do you want to be perfect, lacking in nothing? (James 3:1-18). Unfortunately, because we view perfection as living a sinless life, we brush it off as unreachable. But throughout Scripture Jesus clearly calls us to be perfect. The key to determining the degree of such perfection lies in the words we speak. What comes out of our mouths exposes what is in our hearts. Listen to your words. Are they positive or negative? Before a word pops out of your mouth, it first has had to have been a thought in your heart. If our thoughts are positive, our speech and actions will also be positive. James says that if we have power over our tongue (which is controlled by our thoughts) we will have power over our whole body (James 3:2). Do you pay attention to the thoughts that are hidden in your heart? Do you see a heart full of love and faith, or a heart full of doubt and fear?

## Negativity creates double-mindedness

Why it is that we have a double mind? Is it because we are gaining our identity from a mixture of both positive and negative imagery? *"For what ever is in your heart determines what you say"* (Matthew 12:34 NLT). Our words are tell-tale signs that our hearts may be divided. Our mouths speak bitter and sweet all in the same sentence. Sometimes we bless God, at other times we curse those who are made in his image (James 3:9-12). Such double-mindedness will cause us to become unstable (James 1:8).

> *We cannot find our true selves whilst remaining in our negative mind set.*

## The devil's chat room

God is our true source of strength and, if we focus on him, he will protect us from all double-mindedness. The enemy seeks to distract our eyes from our source of strength by desecrating our minds with depressing imagery. In revenge towards God's plan for us to reflect Jesus, the devil infiltrates our minds with negative messages that are sent from the pit of hell. From his chat room satan reaches into society with his tentacles of lies, criticism, gossip and bitter judgments and entangles our hearts and minds with discouragement, confusion and despair. Such attitudes contaminate our minds like a virus. When a virus infects our bodies we become sick and listless. Or think of the effect a virus has on a computer. The whole system can completely shut down and, unless retrieved, valuable information is destroyed.

Destructive imagery is a hidden but powerful weapon the enemy uses to defame our identity. Just as lethal gases that are odourless are dangerous, so also negativity becomes dangerous because we are often unaware of the effect it has in polluting our minds.

Whatever we fill our minds with will become magnified within us. If an acquaintance comes and complains to you about your friend, and you believe what is said, your imagination kicks in and you see your friend differently than how you did before the conversation. Such is the power of harmful words that can latch onto our imagination. If we believe what we hear we open the door for those words to penetrate our imagination. Have you noticed that negative people can cause you also to become negative?

*Our emotions are often a sign or symptom of deeper issues*

The enemy uses our imagination as a place where he can download an unending source of lies and negative images. Our imagination (or heart) becomes fertile soil where he can plant a lie. If we think too much about that lie it can twist our mind and cripple us emotionally. We can become paranoid as the lie lurks waiting to become real in our lives. This causes us to suffer intolerable pain as we entertain the lies in our imagination. We often suffer there more than we do in real life.

Take for example that day at the manhole when as a child I began my marathon run from evil. Even though, according to Psalm 91, the words spoken that day had no power to harm me, they certainly lead me astray. It was my own interpretation of the lie that created a false impression of who I was. This delusion did not exist in the real world, but only in my mind.

Allowing negative pictures to fill our imagination becomes the basis for many of our fears. Negativity will darken our thoughts and will have a profound affect in distorting out identity. Just as a computer is designed to receive compatible information to the hard drive, so our hearts and minds are also designed for information that will help, not hinder us.

Negativity makes us irritable and is one of the main causes of self-pity. Living from a pessimistic mindset complicates our world, robs our joy and depletes our strength. Negativity feeds phobias and creates a sense of pending disaster. By filling our minds with harmful thoughts we become depressed, confused, discouraged and withdrawn. We lose our sense of vision and worth. A pessimistic attitude destroys our peace and prevents us believing that God is good. Such lies have power to create a dark atmosphere that causes us to grope about and stumble.

The cinema, the tabloids and the music industry are full of negative and destructive images. Negativity has pervaded the work place, our friendships and homes. If we don't block its influence, it can shape our response to offence and determine our reaction to trouble. Our minds were never designed to be cluttered with negativity. We must learn to protect ourselves from the mind pervading viruses that install lies and fear into our lives.

## *Identification*

What goes into our minds determines what comes out of our mouths. Television is a common source of negative images and is watched by billions of people. These images along with song lyrics can go straight into our minds. If we put rubbish into our minds similar rubbish will come out of our mouths.

The battle that rages within our mind has a lot to do with the rubbish that we think about. If we sow fear inspiring images into our minds, the enemy then has a right to attack us using that imagery. Feeding our minds on negativity provides us with little resources to fall back on when facing real problems in the real world.

When caught in a realm of negativity, it is easy to imagine

what we hear and see on the screen happening to us. Everyday we see the effects that destructive images have on social behaviour. I met Andrew a couple of years ago; although very talented, he severely doubted his worth. He grew up in an emotional war zone, he constantly was bullied at school and easily became angry. He tried to escape his anger through drugs and alcohol. (Others do it through work, shopping, or endless coffees). One day, alone and away from family and friends, he watched a violent movie. This sparked fireworks within him that exploded in the pub that night and now he faces two accounts of assault.

## Imagination

The power of negativity creates within us a sense of uneasiness and pervading doom. Having a negative perspective can plunge us into a realm of fear and anxiety; it can cramp our style and prevent us living life to the full. I felt this was happening to my friend Abigail. Twelve months ago I sat with her having coffee. At that time her life was far from good. Everything that possibly could go wrong had gone wrong for her. She was homeless and unemployed. Yet, as I prayed, God gave me a vision of his intervention. Within six months I saw, in the vision, her situation change dramatically, and it did. But just the other day I met with her. Although now married, with a full time job and a beautiful unit to live in, she was still unhappy. Over coffee it became apparent that Abigail was still miserable. Even though her circumstances had changed her negative mindset hadn't.

## Maze of negativity

God has a perfect view of our worth but the mirrors of the world all play their part in preventing us from seeing that beautiful picture. When we are unable to see our true worth we become locked into a maze of doubt. A maze has been described as a "complex network of paths or passages."[42] These paths are surrounded by unyielding walls of circumstance or attitudes that lock us into our lonely world. Rejection, isolation and jealousy, or even a long term illness can become to us walls preventing us from moving forward. We try to push our walls down but the harder we try the more resistant they become.

> *Having a negative perspective can plunge us into a realm of fear and anxiety.*

Are you locked into attitudes of fear, despair, hopelessness, or a lifestyle of addiction where you find no way of escape? Have you found your situation escalating out of control? We simplify our approach to life when we remove all forms of negativity in our thinking.

## Consider

- What are tentacles of negativity?
- How can they reach into society?
- How can lies control our emotions?
- Have you allowed negativity to intimidate and diminish your worth?

My house has many mirrors hanging on its walls.
I go to them most every day
for they will tell me all.

Now each reflect my yearning
of how I want to be
all prettied up and good and sweet
so all the world will see.

But there's a special mirror
that hangs blank upon the wall
and I am strangely drawn to it
it means the most of all.

It gives no outward sign to me,
no flattery there I'll see,
and yet it calls and beckons me
to seeks its mystery.

I gaze upon it when I'm sad,
when self-worth has let me down,
when praise and adoration
become empty clanging sounds.

And as I keep on gazing there
my eyes now see it all.
The mystery that beckoned me
is the reflection of my Lord.

He looks at all my shame and sin,
the masks that hides my sham.
But he will only see my heart
and love me as I am.

The mirrors are all gone now,
I don't need them any more,
for now I'm only looking to
my Saviour and my Lord.

By Pat Bower

# Nineteen

# Restored

*For where is the wrath of the oppressor?*
*The cowering prisoners will soon be set free;*
*they will not die in their dungeon*
*They will not lack bread.*
(Isaiah 51:13-14 NIV)

*But if you look carefully*
*into the perfect law that sets you free,*
*and if you do what it says*
*and don't forget what you heard,*
*then God will bless you for doing it.*
(James 1:22-25 TLT)

*I can't tell you how much I long for you to enter this wide-open, spacious life. We didn't fence you in. The smallness you feel comes from within you. Your lives aren't small, but you're living them in a small way.*[43]

*I*n our first two years of marriage, Brian was teaching at a one-teacher school, and we were living in the school residence at the base of a beautiful mountain near Mudgee. We had been married only eighteen months when we had decided to buy a house in our home town and rent the property.

As we were moving towards fulfilling our desire to own a home, Brian woke up one morning and told me that he was resigning and that we were going to Bible College. He had already made up his mind. Needless to say we didn't buy our house, but instead used our savings for college.

I enjoyed Bible college and the issues were never raised regarding my identity problems; so I felt comfortable and fitted in. You see, deep down in my heart I was I lost. I was saved because I had accepted Jesus, but I had never found my true place of belonging. I had no idea who I was and I didn't know that the Bible could help me find my way back to the person God originally made me to be.

I was a reasonably good student and answered questions with a certain amount of insight. I studied Greek and even got credits in external Greek exams. Each year I memorised hundreds of Bible verses. Sadly in the four years I was at college, I rarely allowed those verses to change my life.

I graduated from Bible college with a distinction. I remember the day well. I was walking back from the lecture block, just before lunch and I told God that I still didn't know who I was. Nor did I know whether he loved me or not. My time at Bible college made me realise that we don't get extra points from God for knowing what is in the Bible. If we look into the mirror and then forget what we look like, we deceive ourselves. In other words, James is saying that if we read the Scriptures and forget to make them real in our situations, we are fooling ourselves (James 1: 22- 25). Often we have our Bible open, yet we don't know how to translate what God has said to us into our everyday lives.

Because we forget who we are, we often become knotted inside with constant worry. Has fear constricted your ability to step out into something new? We cannot find our true selves whilst remaining in our negative mind-set. To become all that God made us to be we need to change the data on which we feed our minds.

*He lifts us from our maze by telling us the truth about our worth.*

Although many are searching for a way of escape, the maze of spiritual darkness has no ground level exits. It is only as we look to God will he reach down and lift us out from our maze. He lifts us from our maze by telling us the truth about our worth. Throughout Scripture God places many signposts that point us towards our true identity. These signposts take the form of divine promises. We have been given promises that firstly enable us to take part in the divine nature and, that secondly, have creative power to change our world (2 Peter 1:4).

## Divine nature is ours

The first divine promise that we need to take note of is that we have been given the DNA of God. We are his children and carry his genes within us. "Through the new birth we become bona fide members of the original cosmic family (Ephesians 3:15), actual generated sons of God (1 John 3:2), partakers of the divine nature (2 Peter 1:4), begotten by Him, impregnated with His "genes", called the seed or "sperma" of God (1 John 5:1, 18 and 1 Peter 1:3, 23), and bearing his heredity."[44]

Alongside receiving God's nature, we have been given other promises. We have been rescued from the kingdom of darkness and have been translated into a kingdom of light (Colossians 1: 13). The veil over our heart has been removed (2 Cor 3:16). We were chosen to be conformed to the image of Jesus (Ephesians 1:4). We have been given the fullness of Christ (Colossians 2:10) and have the ability to see God's goodness (2 Corinthians 4:6). Our sins have been forgiven and the written code of the law, with all its demands, has been nailed to the cross (Colossians 2: 14-15).

> *As you read God's Word Jesus will gently speak to you and restore your tattered image.*

"*With promises like this to pull us on, dear friends, let's make a clean break with everything that defiles or distracts us, both within and without.*"[45] We need to ask ourselves whether we have traded these God given promises by looking into the mirror of negativity. If we do, we will never fully experience God's power and freedom in our lives.

## *Unrestricted freedom*

In battling an identity crisis, God intercepts Job's self-focus and re-directs him to a place of hope. "*God is leading you away from danger, Job, to a place free from distress*" (Job 36:16 NLT). Like Job, I found that as I believed the truth I was re-directed to a spacious and safe place which was full of unrestricted freedom. But to get to this place of safety we need to end all negative thinking and think positive thoughts (Philippians 4:8).

# The power of the Word

Absolute truth is a weapon that destroys the devil's lies. For truth to shape our identity we need to understand how it relates to us personally. When we read God's Word does it automatically penetrate our spirit through a process of osmosis? Unfortunately, it doesn't. We are transformed only to the extent that we act on what God says. Acting on the truth:

- removes the blindfolds from our minds
- enables us to see with our internal eyes
- transforms information from facts to revelation
- empowers the Word to change our lives.

But how do we act on the truth?

> *My child, pay attention to what I say,*
> *Listen carefully to my words.*
> *Don't lose sight of them.*
> *Let them **penetrate deep** into your heart,*
> *For they bring life to those who find them*
> *And healing to their whole body.*
> (Proverbs 4:20-22 NLT)

When we allow God's Word to penetrate the hardened barriers of our heart, we experience breakthrough. God's Word is a hammer that breaks the rock. *"Is not my word like a fire,"* declares the Lord, *"and like a hammer that breaks a rock in pieces?"* (Jeremiah 23:29 NIV). Use the Word to smash the hard places in your life. How much of his Word do we really pay attention to? Do we use the Word to destroy our negative emotions? When the Word affects our emotions we become an impenetrable force against the enemy.

The test as to whether the Word is causing the inner structure of our lives to become strong is found in our responses to daily life. Are we trusting God and becoming an immovable tree, or do we trust man? Are we being swayed like a reed?

God's Word informs us of who we are and where we are going; it reveals our identity. When you look into the mirror of God's Word, do you see that you are righteous, accepted, loved and chosen? We are eternally accepted. Does this truth allow us to walk in peace when our world is falling apart? If we haven't lost sight of this truth, when we are rejected, we will still believe we are completely accepted by God.

Jesus has rescued us from the kingdom of death (Ephesians 2:1). When faced with our own mortality acting on this truth creates within our minds an image that we are in fact invincible.

We read that we are saved by grace (Ephesians 2:8). What does this really mean to us? Do we imagine ourselves living in a kingdom of love in which nothing makes us afraid? Do we use that grace to please God in all things, or do we still want our own way in life? We rebuild our identity when we allow God's Word to impact and transform our circumstances. Rather than merely reading God's Word as a daily ritual, we need to engage with God and ask him questions. We should tell him our doubts and receive his personal revelation concerning us.

Liz had an amazing revelation of grace when God spoke to her. She writes:

Grace
Is not stagnant
Is ever reaching, all consuming
And conquerors sin.
I am Holy
I stir the waters of your soul
And draw you near to me.
Yes, even in your brokenness

I draw you in
From my presence you cannot hide-
Even in the darkest parts
I reach you.
There is nothing My grace cannot overcome
My love for you
Will never cease.

If only we knew the longing in God's heart to draw us close. Circumstances may tell us that God is against us but if we draw near to God, he will set us free from every doubt and fear by telling us the truth. Do you feel vulnerable in certain circumstances? Then listen to the Word, *"Let the beloved of the Lord dwell secure in him, for he shields him all day long and the one the Lord loves rests between his shoulders"* (Deuteronomy 33:12 NIV). It is only as our hearts are opened to his Word that he will be able to transform us into his image.

Do you really see yourself as one who is blameless? Before the foundation of the world God choose us. *"And even before then, he chose us that we might be blameless in his sight"* (Ephesians 1:4 NIV). Blameless carries with it the idea of being unblemished, faultless and without reproach.[47] Such an image is the basis of our true identity.

## *God's Word - a defence against lies*

The truth explains to us what actually is happening. That's why it is good to get God's perspective. When I hear God's ever so gentle whisper, fear-inspiring imagery is destroyed.

As you look to God, he will wash the filth of negativity from you. He will lift you from your maze by re-interpreting your circumstances with his perspective. Hearing God's voice will shape an even clearer image of himself into your identity. As you read God's Word allow it to gently speak to you and rebuild your battered image. As you allow the truth to penetrate your spirit you will discover an image of glory being shaped into your life. In God's eyes you are beautiful. God desires to raise you up from the ashes of your own doubts and transform you with his encouraging words. The words of Jesus are liquid love and are able to restore our true character.

It is vital that we understand the words of God are not ordinary words. Jesus refers to his words as "spirit and life." His word is "*alive and powerful. It is sharper than any two edged sword, cutting between soul and spirit, between joint and marrow. It exposes our inner most thoughts and desires*" (Hebrews 4:12 NLT). Able to penetrate the depth of our thoughts, God's Word has ability to get into the deep crevices of our minds. It is there in our minds that the water of the Word washes off every trace of negativity that mars our beautiful image. As you read God's Word Jesus will gently speak to you and restore your tattered image. The truth becomes a rock that builds secure lives.

> *He will lift you from your maze by re-interpreting your circumstances with his perspective.*

"*The words I speak to you are not incidental additions to your life, home owner improvements to your standard of living. They are foundational words, words to build your life on. If you work these words into your life, you are like a smart carpenter who built his house on solid rock. Rain poured down, the river flooded, a tornado hit – but nothing moved that house. It was fixed to the rock.*"[46]

Because we become what we think, it is vital that God's Word alone influences the way we see ourselves (Matthew 9:29). If we allow the Holy Spirit to fill our imagination with God's Word, then our likeness will be transformed from a kitten into a courageous conquering lion. It is only as we fill our imagination with imagery from God that we will be transformed into his likeness.

> *And we, who with unveiled faces*
> *All reflect the Lord's glory,*
> *Are being transformed into his likeness*
> *With ever-increasing glory,*
> *Which comes from the Lord,*
> *who is spirit.* (2 Corinthians 3:18 NIV)

In making the Word of God relevant to our situations old thought patterns, that were programmed into our mind when we lived independently of God, are dismantled. Understanding how God's Word relates to our ordinary moments better equips us to combat lies. Believing that God has all the answers to life's perplexities enables us to live in continual victory. As we look into the perfect mirror that shines light onto our identity we will see a deep clear view of our worth.

## Damaged walls

The enemy uses offence and trouble to damage the walls, or thought patterns, that would normally protect our heart. Rather than feeling protected, a damaged wall will expose us to the brunt of the storm. If we don't think according to how God thinks, then we may feel like our lives are being lashed by continual storms.

> *O afflicted city, lashed by storms*
> *and not comforted,*

*I will build you with stones of turquoise,*
*your foundations with sapphires.*
*I will make your battlements of rubies,*
*Your gates of sparkling jewels*
*and all your walls of precious stones.*
*All your sons will be taught by the Lord*
*And great will be your children's peace*
*In righteousness you will be established.*
*Tyranny will be far from you:*
*you will have nothing to fear.*
(Isaiah 54:11-14 NIV)

In ancient times walls were built around the cities to protect them from invasions. These walls gave the people room to live and roam within its wide confines. Truth, when believed, has supernatural power to build protective walls around our lives preventing the enemy access. These walls shield and defend our image. The enemy targets these walls with lies. As we destroy these lies, satan's violent insinuations and destructive insults will no longer be heard by the antennas of our heart. Instead we will hear words that reveal our true beauty.

> *God's Word will build strong fortifying walls around our lives.*

God has given us many promises in his Word that tell us who we are. If we allow these promises to form our identity, we become what they say. Every time we make the Word of God relevant to our situation we place another jewel in the wall of our heart. By allowing our identity to be shaped into the image of God we become strong. Applying relevant Scripture verses to our situation, builds strong fortifying walls around our lives. *"The walls that you are rebuilding are never out of my sight.*

*Your builders are faster than your wreckers. The demolition crews are gone for good."*

Do you know who you are? This liberty bell captures a summary of our true identity.

I KNOW WHO I AM
I am God's child (John 1:12)
I am Christ's friend (John 15:15)
I am united with the Lord(1 Cor. 6:17)
I am bought with a price(1 Cor 6:19-20)
I am a saint (set apart for God). (Eph. 1:1)
I am a personal witness of Christ (Acts 1:8)
I am the salt & light of the earth (Matt.5:13-14)
I am a member of the body of Christ (1 Cor 12:27)
I am free forever from condemnation (Rom. 8: 1-2)
I am a citizen of Heaven. I am significant ( Phil.3:20)
I am free from any charge against me (Rom. 8:31-34)
I am a minister of reconciliation for God(2 Cor.5:17-21)
I have access to God through the Holy Spirit (Eph. 2:18)
I am seated with Christ in the heavenly realms (Eph. 2:6)
I cannot be separated from the love of God(Rom.8:35-39)
I am established, anointed, sealed by God (2 Cor.1:21-22)
I am assured all things work together for good (Rom. 8: 28)
I have been chosen and appointed to bear fruit (John 15:16)
I may approach God with freedom and confidence (Eph. 3: 12)
I can do all things through Christ who strengthens me (Phil. 4:13)
I am the branch of the true vine, a channel of His life (John 15: 1-5)
I am God's temple (1 Cor. 3: 16). I am complete in Christ (Col. 2: 10)
I am hidden with Christ in God (Col. 3:3). I have been justified (Romans5:1)
I am God's co-worker (1 Cor. 3:9; 2 Cor 6:1). I am God's workmanship (Eph. 2:10)
I am confident that the good works God has begun in me will be perfected (Phil. 1: 5)
I have been redeemed and forgiven (Col. 1:14). I have been adopted as God's child (Eph 1:5)
I belong to God

Have you built any of these truths into the wall of your heart? The more we believe these truths, the more God is able to build up our walls surrounding our heart. When we learn to apply the Word of God to our lives we then live under the full blessing and protection of heaven.

*"Blessed are those who have learned to acclaim you, who walk in the light of your presence, O Lord. They rejoice in your name all day long; they exalt in your righteousness,*

*for you are their glory and their strength, and by your favour you exalt our horn, indeed our shield belongs to the Lord, our king to the Holy One of Israel"*
(Psalm 89:15-18 NIV).

Our true identity is restored as we fix our thoughts on God and his Word. Embracing our true image allows us to reflect back to the world unexplainable peace and courage in the midst of adverse circumstances.

## Consider

- What vision do you have of your identity?
- Truth is a light that reveals to us what we look like in God's eyes. Explain.

  Explain how truth enables you to:
  - combat lies
  - dismantle old thought patterns
  - live in continual victory.

# Twenty

# *An Identity Worth Dying For*

*I sought the Lord, and he answered me;*
*he delivered me from all my fear.*
*Those who look to him are radiant;*
*their faces are never covered with shame.*
(Psalm 34:4-5 NIV)

# Need of forgiveness

*A*re you struggling with personal guilt, feeling condemned by past failures? The deepest cry of the human heart is to be known intimately and still be loved. Essentially this cry is a deep need to experience a forgiveness that reaches into the core of our being. Some of us live with profound unbelief in God's goodness and love because we cannot forgive ourselves for things that we have done in the past. We use logical reasoning believing that if we do something wrong we will be punished. We even shut God out of particular areas of our lives, fearing that he would reject us if he knew certain things about us. God knows everything ... even our secrets. Our ways and thoughts are known to him. When we understand that he already has intimate knowledge of our entire lives we may better understand the depth of his forgiveness.

God cares about what is happening on the inside of our hearts and knows when we are able, or unable, to accept his forgiveness. He understands with tender compassion and embraces us with acceptance. Very few of us actually grasp that we are loved that much. Yet, we are loved that much and Jesus, who deeply values our worth, died to restore us back to himself.

The death and resurrection of Jesus is the centre point of eternity. He died and rose again that we might be acquitted. Throughout Scripture God assures us that we are forgiven. Yet many times we think there are hidden clauses preventing us receiving that forgiveness. Maybe we think that our sin is too big and that Jesus death doesn't cover it. If we can't forgive ourselves we become inward, self-obsessed and easily succumb to negativity and the rejection of others. Not understanding that we are totally forgiven for our past failures is one of the main causes of anxiety, depression and deep loneliness.

Do you experience peace or are you angry with yourself? If we don't like ourselves, we not only develop bondage of self-hatred, but we will give the enemy a foothold to our lives. *"Do not the let the sun go down while you are still angry. And do not give the devil a foothold"* (Ephesians 4: 26-27 NIV).

We have inherited a natural bent towards doing the wrong thing. Throughout our lives some of us have lived for the here and now and have built our identity on what is physical rather than spiritual. Yet, deep down we know that we are accountable to a higher being. This knowledge is inbuilt within each of us. So even though we may have lived a self-focused life, we still search for the perfect stain remover to make us feel clean inside.

*If we can't forgive ourselves we become inward, self-obsessed and easily succumb to negativity and the rejection of others.*

If we don't understand that Jesus' death is the perfect stain remover we will hold ourselves at arm's length to God's forgiveness. At home one day I noticed that my doona cover had a deeply ingrained black mark on it. Not actually believing that anything could shift that mark, I sprayed it with the toughest of stain removers. To my delight the stain vanished before my eyes. But what was even more astonishing was that the stain instantly transferred onto my hands and made them black. Jesus spoke quietly to my heart and said that in the same way my sin instantly transferred onto him and made his body black with death.

My sin, whether it is past, present or future has been forever cancelled at the cross. The words spoken by Jesus, ***"It is finished"*** speaks of the finality of the payment of our sin (John 19:30).

*God made him who had no sin to be sin for us,*

*so that in him we might become*
*the righteousness of God.* (2 Corinthians 5:21 NIV)

In bearing our sin Jesus, not only opened a door in heaven to the Father's heart, he also made a way for us to see our original identity. Accepting this truth is the bridge we all must cross to attain true self-acceptance.

Years ago Jesus spoke into my life concerning the importance of forgiving myself. He said, "I have taken away your sin at Calvary. Continue to come to me for cleansing and don't forget to claim my total forgiveness. The matter is then settled. Never to be raised again. When you allow fear to lurk around each corner, rebuke it, reminding it that your sin has forever been forgiven. Satan's forces gain a hold on you by getting you to look at past weakness. Instead, look at the strengths that you have in me. My strength will become more and more part of your life as you feast on all that I am. Forget about yourself. Look to me totally for your life. Draw strength from all that I am. Continue to rest and cease all struggles."

*"Guilt is banished through love and truth."*[51] Even though our sin is an offence to God, it does not alter his love towards us. Even when I am conscious of my sin, Jesus appears to be unaffected by what I have done. It isn't that he doesn't care that sin is an affront to his holiness and provokes pain in his heart. He does care and this is why he wants us to stay away from destructive behaviour. Does Jesus want us to repent and discover a new way of behaving? Yes, of course, but he does not walk away from us or strike out in anger. Instead he is gentle; having no need to retaliate, having already obliterated our sin at the cross.

If we think God condemns us, we will close our hearts to him. At the Cross Jesus smashed the mirror of sin and death and broke the chains that kept us slaves to sin. He offers us a divine exchange, holding out before us the mirror of grace. If we look into this mirror we won't feel condemned. An acronym for grace is *God's Riches At Christ's Expense*. God's riches are given to us on the basis of faith. Knowing we are forgiven prevents us going insane and helps us to forget about ourselves.

When we sin Jesus is there to forgive us, thereby smashing all perceived judgements that society may make of us. Jesus doesn't reject us when we fail him, rather he shares his goodness with us. He does not turn his back when we need him the most. Instead of being angry Jesus embraces us and keeps his heart open. The embrace of God reinforces our infinite worth. In my mind's eye I have seen his gentleness warming my heart. His grace, when we need it the most, is what brings us close to him. His compassion and readiness to accept us is not dependent on our behaviour. His mercy reaches to our darkest secret and uncovers the shroud of shame that has hidden our beautiful inner self.

## *Freedom*

God desires to bring complete healing into our lives. Receiving God's healing power sets us free to become the people we are destined to be. But we have to open our hearts and be honest. *"Where the spirit of the Lord is there is freedom"* (2 Corinthians 3:17 NIV). Such liberty gives us the ability to agree with God on attitudes that affect our personal behaviour. When we become upset we can ask God to show us the lie we believe that is making us fearful, or the idol we are protecting. Fears of abandonment or punishment, rejection or self-hatred may be the root cause of many sins that we struggle with. As we embraced by God's forgiveness, we are then able to deal with and overcome the deceptions and idolatry that provoke us to sin.

Jesus paid a high price so that God the Father can totally embrace and accept us. God is very gentle as he reveals to us why we allow the devil to affect our identity. When we hear God's gentle whisper concerning our wilful attitudes, we are then able to live free from sin.

Realising that God is willing to rescue us allows us to open ourselves up for him to tenderly restore our lives. If we are controlled by the way God sees us then we will want to do the right thing and will make choices that take us away from sin. Understanding that we are totally forgiven and that God has given us his Spirit makes the Christian life easy to live.

## Toxic shame

We may be able to forgive ourselves for things we have done wrong, but what about the things that we haven't done and yet are blamed for? Does Jesus death cover that? Maybe an injustice, an abuse or harsh treatment has caused us to feel that we are bad to the core of our being. We torment ourselves as we try to work out why we were abandoned or abused or why that horrible situation occurred.

Vanessa survived two violent marriages believing that the violence against her was that of her own doing. She believed that it was her fault. Shaun was abandoned on a park bench when he was three years old. He now hides his pain behind an addictive lifestyle. Suzanne's mother walked out on her when she was six weeks old. These traumatic experiences have had power to etch shame deep into their hearts. They crave being forgiven for stuff they not responsible for. Many others who have been mistreated have also desired to be restored to a feeling of wholeness or completeness.

## Shame distorts our image

Shame has tremendous power in distorting our image. Craig Hill in *Ancient Paths* says, "Shame is a deep, deep wound of being that is a result of the cursing of identity. Shame, as opposed to guilt, is a deep feeling of wrongness of BEING. Guilt on the other hand, is a feeling of wrongness of ACTION. Guilt says, 'I made a mistake,' shame says, 'I AM a mistake.'"[52] Craig then goes on to explain that we can be forgiven for things we have done wrong but we cannot be forgiven if we are a mistake. He says, "Shame is a deep feeling of contamination, uncleanness, and of being uniquely flawed. It causes us to feel inept, different and isolated from others."[5]

> *We are in a war over our image and it is vital we become aware of situations that make us feel rejected and unloved.*

Shame begins at that place of being embarrassed, wounded or rejected by someone important to us. Shame is then reinforced by our unforgiving attitude both towards our offender and ourselves. At the point of humiliation we question our worth. Shame defames us and slanders our worth. We are in a war over our image and it is vital we become aware of situations that make us feel rejected and unloved. When we live in an arena of shame our feelings will constantly lie and bring confusion. Have we felt guilty because we were treated badly and now we blame ourselves for circumstances that were not our fault? When we are made to feel accountable for what others have done to us it becomes hard to accept ourselves. The person responsible for inflicting the wound is made to look innocent and the wounded is made to look guilty. Thin webs of demonic imagery entangle many fragile lives by implied or transferred guilt.

To the extent that we experience the scars of guilt we lack confidence to become our true selves. The masks that we wear become the walls that we live behind. Addictive lifestyles are a common way to hide inferiority and guilt. People who destroy their lives on drugs, promiscuous sex and alcoholic binges are often plagued with deep sense of worthlessness.

But this is exactly the plan of the enemy. If he can get us to hate ourselves he knows that we will reject God's view of us. Many nurse their wounds and spend the rest of their lives curled up in an emotional huddle. Sure, the ego might get up and fight a few battles and some may make something reasonable of their life, but the true inner eternal self lies wounded on the sidelines.

It is important that we fight shame-inspiring imagery as we would a virus, because if we don't like ourselves, we will become self-absorbed and reflect a bad attitude. God knows about the pain in our hearts. He gently asks us to come out from behind our walls. He whispers our name and invites us to bring our wounds to him. If we have the courage to come out from behind our walls and be honest, we will discover that not only does he heal our hearts, but he also imparts a new fresh vision of our true worth.

## Jesus heals our wounds

Receiving God's mercy is essential if we are to accept ourselves. If life has ripped us off and stolen things that were once precious, we can ask Jesus to breathe life into the very thing that we once cherished. Maybe it is a place where you last saw your Mum? Maybe you never met your Dad? God wants to wipe your tears and heal the ache in your heart that is causing you to despise yourself. It is not your fault that you were abandoned, mistreated or abused. God wants to take you up as his child and become both Mum and Dad to you.

Maybe your dreams died when you first got involved in drugs or when you lost your virginity to a casual friend. It was at this place that you gave up on life. Take Jesus there. Take him to that place where your heart was broken and your dreams were stolen. Take Jesus to the place where memories of abuse and rejection have been buried in cold, dark emotional tombs. Allow Jesus to roll away that stone that covers, up the shame hidden in your heart. Whatever the situation that caused your hurt, disappointment and grief, God wants to breathe his life into the hopes and dreams that have died. No longer will you believe that God expects you to be more than you are. You will experience his healing. He loves you.

We can become our own best friend when we experience the healing touch of Jesus. As we accept ourselves, we will experience incredible peace and strength. Rather than being downcast, our faces will become radiant; rather than blushing with shame, we will be confident.

> *Instead of their shame they will receive a double portion, instead of their disgrace, they will rejoice in their inheritance so they will inherit a double portion.* (Isaiah 61:7 NIV)

Whatever message the enemy has scribbled over our tender hearts, the cross replaces that message with infinite value. When our identity becomes clear in our minds we will reflect the unlimited peace residing within the heart of God.

Believing the truth imparts peace and controls the way we feel (Colossians 3:15). God's peace is so powerful that it has the ability to still the storms that rage within our minds. Isaiah 26:3 states that if we keep our mind focused on God we will enter into perfect peace. Only as we make the truth relevant will we become an unstoppable force against the powers of darkness.

## Consider

- Have you experienced God's tenderness when you have failed him?
- We resist the enemy's tactics when we bring our wounds to Jesus. Why do you think this is true?
- Do you find it easy to forgive yourself?

Since I didn't
understand
my true worth
the offence
placed
my fragile identity
at
further risk.

# Twenty One

# Lifted

*Here is a simple, rule-of-thumb*
*guide for behaviour:*
*Ask yourself,*
*What do you want people to do for you,*
*then grab the initiative*
*and do it for them.*[54]

*But you shall be perfect just*
*as your heavenly father is perfect.*
(Matthew 5:48 NKJV)

*T*he real test to see how much we have forgiven ourselves is seen in our willingness to forgive others. The enemy often uses those closest to us to wound our soul. It is those who we care about the most that have the greatest power to hurt us. And when they do, we may find it really hard to forgive. Instead of being patient we usually throw these people out of our lives, wishing not to see them again.

This attitude does not reflect the heart of God who welcomes and loves us unconditionally. Jesus says in Matthew 18:22 that we are to forgive the same person at least five hundred times a day. However, in misunderstanding this verse, we can assume it means that people can hurt us in any way they like and it is our job to forgive.

There was a time in my life when I allowed people to treat me anyway they pleased. Forgiving others does not mean we have to continually place ourselves in situations where we can be hurt. Nor does it mean that we must become a doormat so people can treat us badly. Forgiveness is born out of a willingness to place value on people, no matter how they behave.

Peter, one of the twelve disciples, became fearful and denied even knowing Jesus at the crucifixion. But in Jesus darkest hour when everyone had fled, Jesus still kept the vision of Peter as being the rock on which he would build his church. During a fireside breakfast, Jesus reinstated Peter and restored him back into his inner circle.

Often we refuse to restore those who have hurt us back into our circle of friendship. I have heard it said, "I have forgiven, but I will never forget what that person did to me." When we give mental assent that we should forgive, but hold onto the offence, we fail to pardon the injustice.

"*A brother offended is harder to win than a strong city*" (Proverbs 18:19 NKJV). Are you that person? Maybe there is someone who has intentionally or unintentionally wounded you and now you have put the brick walls up so high that they are impenetrable. God desires that your heart be healed.

My aim is to inspire love for those who inflicted pain even if resolution is not possible. There are some serious consequences if we cannot maintain a readiness to forgive:

- we will not feel forgiven by God (Matthew 6:14-15)
- a root of bitterness will spring up within us and we will defile those about us (Hebrews 12:15)
- we will be tormented (Matthew 12:15).

Therefore God desires that we make a life of forgiving others a priority. Forgiving means that we first destroy intimidating messages that offend our hearts. It is only when our identity is not at jeopardy that we can love and forgive others.

> *Affirming another's worth enables me to forgive and forget the past.*

The devil works hard at sending messages that make us feel unlovely and worthless. Yet we can outsmart him by finding our true worth. When we see our own worth it is easier to believe the best about others.

The choice to forgive becomes easier when our damaged identity is healed. Why it is that Jesus inspires us to bless those who curse us, and 'turn the other cheek"? Why does he presume that praying for those who persecute us has become a natural part of our lifestyles? Is it because he assumes that we are not depending on people, and the way they treat us, to tell us a message about ourselves? Jesus expects that if we know who we are then we will want others to know who they truly are.

> *The choice to forgive becomes easier when our damaged identity is healed.*

Having our own image restored and gaining a clear view of our offender's worth gives courage to take our love to another level. We can bless people and pray for them from a distance in the privacy of our own heart. But when we truly know who we are then we can be up front about our love to the point where we are "*kind to those who despitefully use* us" (Matthew 5: 43-48).

"*Contention is like the bars of a castle*" (Proverbs 18:19 NKJV). Arguments can trap us and lock us into hateful attitudes. The wicked servant felt trapped when he realised his creditors were chasing him. However, he wasn't locked up because he was forgiven the debt. The parable of the wicked servant[55] illustrates God's response to those who are forgiven but don't take the time to erase their own negative self-images. The wicked servant found it hard to forgive because he failed to see himself as forgiven. He carried in his heart old distorted images of one who owed a lot of money. If he had accepted that he was no longer in debt he would have more easily been able to forgive those who were in debt to him.

In the past I have found it really hard to forgive because I have never really dealt with the myriad of distorted images given to me when I was offended. I would hold those negative pictures of myself being offended up in my imagination and continually go over them in my mind. Daily I would rehearse the event. Since I didn't understand my true worth the offence placed my fragile identity at further risk. But if, during the process of working towards forgiveness, my identity had been restored and healed then I would have found it easier to forgive. Offence not only gives us opportunity to reflect God's nature it is also an opportunity to discover new aspects of our spiritual DNA.

God is always looking for a perfect man (2 Chronicles16:9) who generously places value and worth on people who seem cruel and nasty. Yet, we can only place value on those who are unkind when we first have a deep clear view of our worth.

## Consider

- Why does offence place our fragile identity at further risk?
- Why it is that Jesus inspires us to bless those who curse us and "turn the other cheek?"
- Why can we only place value on those who seem nasty when we understand our worth?

*Let me tell you why you are here. You're here to be salt –
seasoning that brings out the God–flavours of this earth. If you
lose your saltiness, how will people taste godliness?*

*Here's another way to put it: you're here to be the light, bringing
out the God colours in this world. God is not a secret to be kept.
We're going public with this, as public as a city on a hill.*

*If I make you light bearers, you don't think I'm going to hide you
under a bucket, do you? I'm putting you on a light stand - shine!
Keep open house; be generous with your lives.*[56]

# Twenty Two

# *Walking in the Light*

*Finally all of you should be of one mind. Sympathize with each other. Love each other as brothers and sisters. Be tender-hearted and keep a humble attitude. Don't repay evil for evil. Don't retaliate with insults when people insult you. Instead, pay them back with a blessing. That's what God called you to do, and he will bless you for it. (1 Peter 3: 10 NLT)*

*H*arbouring an offence poisons our attitudes, taints our image and distorts our worth. An unforgiving attitude binds us to the very people and scenarios that have caused us pain. We can know if we have an unforgiving attitude by the amount of time we spend thinking about the person who hurt us or by the amount of time we spend looking back into the past. God desires that we live in the freedom that Jesus won for us at the Cross, and he has given us a strategy to make this possible.

When we sin Jesus doesn't rise up in anger, but he is gentle.

> *An unforgiving attitude binds us to the very people and scenarios that have caused us pain.*

Likewise when someone hurts us by giving us a distorted or cracked view of our worth, Jesus desires that we are patient with that person. We are to place value on them simply because they are made in God's image. "*And be careful when you get on each others nerves don't snap at each other. Look for the best in each other, and always do your best to bring it out.*"[57] Surely if God is the only person who has a right to tell me a message about my worth he also is the only One who should determine our attacker's worth.

## *Forgiveness sets everyone free*

In forgiving, we not only set our offender free from their debt, but we also side-step the traps set for us (Psalm 18:39-40). Making a lifestyle of searching for the treasure in people prevents hateful, bitter judgements developing towards those who hurt us. Remember, the enemy wants to keep us in an unforgiving attitude so that a root of bitterness will entangle our lives and so that we will live in constant torment (Matthew 12:15, 6:14-15, Hebrews 12:15).

As we seek God concerning our offender's worth, we are more able to rise up as an overcomer. Overcoming is directly related to forgiving an offence. We can't overcome an offence if we are full of bitterness and hatred towards our offender.

God's strategy involves asking him for his opinion of those who have hurt us. In order to break the chain and escape my pain we have to find a source of power beyond our natural human abilities. When we are hurt we often define people by the sin they commit against us. For example, if we are hurt by someone's anger we define that person as angry. If we are hurt by their selfishness we define them as selfish. At this point we are walking in darkness because we fail to see that person the way God does.

John, in his letter to the churches, connects an unforgiving attitude with walking in the dark. When we walk into a dark room it is likely we will stumble. If we turn the light on, everything becomes clear.

> *If any one says, "I am living in the light," but hates a Christian brother or sister, that person is still living in darkness. Anyone who loves another brother or sister is living in the light and does not cause anyone to stumble. But anyone who hates a Christian brother or sister is still living and walking in darkness. Such a person does not know the way to go, having been blinded by the darkness.* (1 John 2: 9-11 NLT)

Can you see the direct connection between walking in darkness and not loving our brother? We are made to be a mirror of God's image. God has made us with the same characteristics and qualities as himself. He is light and so are we. "*If I make you light bearers, you don't think I'm going to hide you under a bucket, do you? I'm putting you on a light stand - shine! Keep open house; be generous with your lives.*[58] So that we might fully reach our potential, God calls us out of darkness into *"his marvellous light"* (1 Peter 2:9). Light is only necessary when it is dark. Just as a torch on a dark night makes a difference and kerosene lamp during a blackout makes a difference so too, we are called to make a difference in a dark world. To become light we need to know where to find the switch in our lives.

So how do we turn the light on so that we can see clearly? "Jesus knew that whatever he spoke to would rise up in people ... he speaks to the treasure in people and releases it from captivity to the flesh. He extracts the precious from the worthless."[102] It is only as we ask God for his opinion of those who have hurt us that we are able to walk in the light. The light helps us to see clearly. Like Jesus, we too can ignore the rubbish in people and speak to their treasure. Discovering the treasure in people enables us to be like God who always looks for the treasure in each of us.

> *He led me to a place of safety; he rewarded me because he delights in me. The Lord heard me for doing right. He restored me because of my innocence. For I have kept the ways of the Lord. I have not turned from my God to follow evil.* (Psalm 18: 19-20 NLT)

God desires that we rise up to become people who are courageous, unshakable and invincible. To be such people we need to build into our lives compassion, kindness, humility, gentleness and patience (Colossians 3:12). These qualities, surprisingly enough, help us to get off our high horse of pride and walk with an open heart. Soft hearts that are able to be moulded empower us to overcome life's difficulties.

*"The lips of the wise protect them"* (Proverbs 14:3 NLT). I remember a time when I worked with a group of women who neither appreciated nor understood my gentle nature. In their eyes I was a pushover. They could say whatever they liked and I would not

respond in a harsh manner. But what these women didn't understand was that I had a hotline to heaven. When someone would make a cutting remark I would ask God how he saw that person. I was surprised at his response. Erin had a particularly fiery temper, but God told me he saw a capacity for great gentleness within her. Michelle seemed really tough on the outside, but on the inside God showed me there was a real softness. He told me that when her feelings were hurt she would protect herself with a harsh exterior. God's opinion of our enemy becomes a treasure found in the dark place

> *It is only as we ask God for his opinion of those who have hurt us that we are able to walk in the light.*

of offence. This treasure is the hidden worth of our offender. He will "*give you the treasure of darkness, riches stored in secret places*" (Isaiah 45:3 NIV). A soft answer (even if it is within our mind) turns away wrath.

Has failing to see someone's worth caused you to become blind? Can you see your offender as God sees them? John is very clear, "*If we love our Christian brother or sister it proves we have passed from death to eternal life. But a person who does not love is still dead*" (1 John 3:14 NLT). When we forgive we can feel God's forgiveness for us. We are not tormented by wrong images of ourselves and the root of bitterness has no room to spring up in our lives. Is this who we are? Are we paying people back for what they have done to us or are we walking confidently and boldly? Are we meek when slandered? Are we mostly *gentle* in our relationships? Are we *kind* to those who hurt us and *patient* in the midst of a longstanding frustration? Are we *hopeful* in times of discouragement? By not allowing evil imagery to develop in our hearts concerning another's worth, God restores our innocence.

Our situations become less difficult when we forgive. We

reflect Jesus whenever we love someone who does not deserve our love. Whenever we bless those who curse us we not only reveal Jesus' nature, but we also protect our true image from being bent out of shape. Choosing to believe that we have what we need to live successful lives empowers God to change us. *In a word, what I'm saying is, grow up. You're kingdom subjects. Now live like it. Live out your God-created identity. Live generously and graciously towards others, the way God lives towards you.*[59]

## Consider

- What are the three outcomes of failing to forgive?
- Is there someone you need to forgive?
- What does it mean to forgive from our mind but not from our heart?

# Twenty Three

# Clear Reflection

*For the law of the spirit of life in Christ Jesus*
*has made me free*
*from the law of sin and death.*
(Romans 8:2 NKJV)

Unbelief
prevents us seeing
our value

# Am I truly who God says I am?

The story of a wealthy man and his son who loved to collect rare works of art is worth relating. They had everything in their collection from Picasso to Raphael. They would often sit together and admire the great works of art. The son went off to war where he died in battle while rescuing another soldier. The father grieved deeply for his only son.

About a month later, just before Christmas, there was a knock on the door. A young man stood at the door with a large package in his hand. He said, "Sir you do not know me but I am the soldier for whom your son gave his life. He saved many lives that day and he was carrying me to safety when a bullet struck him in the heart and he died instantly. He often talked about you and your love for art."

The young man held out the package. "I know this isn't much. I am not really a great artist, but I think your son would have wanted you to have this." The father opened the package. It was a portrait of his son painted by the young man. He stared in awe at the way the soldier had captured the personality of his son in the painting. The father was so drawn to the eyes that his own eyes welled up with tears. He thanked the young man and offered to pay him for the painting. "Oh no sir, I could never repay what your son did for me. It is a gift."

The father hung the portrait over his mantle. Every time visitors came to his home, he took them to see the portrait of his son before he showed them any of the other great works he had collected. The man died a few months later. There was to be a great auction of his paintings. Many influential people gathered excited over seeing the great paintings and having an opportunity to purchase one for their collection.

On the platform sat the painting of the son. The auctioneer pounded the gavel. "We will start the bidding with the painting of the son. Who will bid for this painting?" There was silence. Then a voice in the back of the room shouted. "We want to see the famous paintings. Skip this one." But the auctioneer persisted. "Will someone bid for the painting?" Another voice shouted angrily, "We didn't come to see this painting; we came to see the Van Goghs, the Rembrandts. Get on with the real bids," the auctioneer continued, "the son, the son, who will take the son?"

Finally, a voice came from the very back of the room. It was the long time gardener of the man and his son. "I'll give $10 for the painting." Being a poor man it was all he could afford. 'We have $10, who will bid $20?' The crowd was becoming angry. They did not want the picture of the son; they wanted more worthy investments for their collections. The auctioneer pounded his gavel. "Going once, going twice - sold for $10." A man sitting in the second row shouted; "Now let's get on with the collection."

The auctioneer laid down his gavel. "What about the paintings?" cried a man in the front row. "I'm sorry the auction is over. When I was called to conduct the auction I was told of a secret stipulation in the will. Only the painting of the son would be auctioned. Whoever bought the painting would inherit the entire estate, including the paintings. The man who took the son gets everything."[60]

*Likewise when we put our faith in Jesus the whole estate of God's kingdom becomes ours.*

The gardener's poverty didn't prevent him from participating in the auction. With a mere ten dollars and a desire for the treasured painting of the son, the whole estate became his. In our day this could be likened to "getting something for nothing." If something is too good to be true we mostly think there is a hidden catch.

Do you believe that you are a brand new person?

Most of us don't live as if we believe that we are new. Maybe, just maybe, we feel we really haven't got a new nature because somewhere in the fine print (and some Bibles do have 'fine print') there is a hidden catch. For many of us, having a new self, remains too good to be true.

> For as he thinks in his heart, so he is.
> (Proverbs 23:7 KJV)

## The exchanged life

The father gave the whole estate to the person who took the painting of his son. Likewise when we put our faith in Jesus the whole estate of God's kingdom becomes ours.

Within each of us is an imprinted image that reflects a clear view of God. Peter tells us that we share in the divine nature (2 Peter 1:4). Within us lays a spiritual DNA that has all the traits of a wondrous and great God. Hidden deep within our spiritual genetics is an image of a strong, bold and conquering lion. Yet many of us may find it hard to reflect God in the push and shove of daily life. There is a big gap between Genesis 1:26 and who we have now become.

To understand how the new self changes our lives, we need to realise when and where it was that we lost our glory.

Prior to the fall, Adam had within him a brilliant light that gave him insight to the nature of his true worth. With a desire to know *good and evil*, this light was snuffed out and instantly he was surrounded in deep darkness. He stumbled in self-doubt, groping to rediscover the light in which he once walked. In trading his original glory for shame, Adam's sin disconnected us from our true source of identity and opened up the way for the enemy to make us feel ugly, abandoned and insignificant. Adam covering himself with the fig leaves is like us grabbing for the BMW to cover our sense of lack.

*"There is a way of life that looks harmless enough, but look again – it leads straight to hell."*[61] Eating from the tree looked harmless enough, but Adam didn't realise a simple bite would plunge him into a realm of death and destruction. As a runner passes the baton on in a relay race, so Adam has passed the baton of sin onto each of us. Sin has blinded our eyes to the knowledge of God's glory. The Greek work for *glory* is *doxa* and "primarily signifies an opinion, estimate."[62] Instead of God esteeming our worth according to the value he places on us, the lust of fleshly desires, the pride in personal achievements and the quest for knowledge have become the things that determine our identity as we know it today.

> *So justice is far from us, and righteousness does not reach us. We look for light, but all is darkness; for brightness but we walk in deep shadows. Like the blind we grope along the wall, feeling our way like men without eyes. At midday we stumble as if it were twilight; among the strong we are like the dead.* (Isaiah 59: 9-10 NIV)

Sin has prevented us from depending on God alone for our identity. Through our own short sightedness we believe that we are loved provided everything is going our way. To be transformed we need a new perspective.

> *The eye is the lamp of the body.*
> *If your eyes are good, your whole body*
> *will be full of light.*
> *But if your eyes are bad, your whole body*
> *will be full of darkness.*
> *If then the light within you is darkness,*
> *how great is that darkness!* (Matthew 6: 22-23 NIV)

Jesus refers to those who lack perception as having eyes but not being able to see (Matthew 13:15). We see *through* our physical eyes but we also see *with* the inner eyes of our heart. Our inner eyes are the windows of our soul. They enable us to perceive things that would be otherwise hidden from our understanding.

The men who walked with Jesus on the Emmaus road initially lacked perception, but when Jesus broke the bread and gave it to them their eyes were opened and they recognised him (Luke 24:31). Paul prays that the eyes of our heart will be enlightened. Our way of seeing will be good when we understand life from God's perspective. Having a clear understanding of our identity prevents us making the mistake of letting the world tell us who we are.

> *Living from the new self places us in a devil free zone.*

Paul had his eyes opened instantly and by seeing into this new dimension his old self became irrelevant. If we focus on what Jesus has done for us we enter into the place where we can locate our new identity. God gives us the responsibility to reflect his image and he has given us his nature so that we are able to do this. He has placed his Spirit within us so that we can make the right choice in every situation. As Christians, we are told that we should now put on the new self, which is "*being renewed in knowledge in the image of its Creator*" (Colossians 3:10 NIV).

When we put on a coat, we are clothing ourselves with a warm jacket. Likewise when we "put on" love, compassion and forgiveness we are clothing ourselves with our new nature. The more loving we are; the more layers of the new self we put on and the less room the enemy will have to determine our image.

# Law of sin

We have been set free from the law of sin and death. It is a done deal. Yet, the enemy uses our sense of worthlessness as a trap to allure us back into bondage. If we don't believe that we have worth, the law of sin will control our lives. The law of sin and death locks us into the past. This law states that if you sin you will be condemned. If we are living under this law, we will naturally focus on our sin and we will feel condemned! The more we feel condemned, the more we will be inclined to do the wrong thing! Have you noticed that guilt keeps us focused on the wrong thing that we have done.

## The law of grace

*"You, however, are controlled not by the sinful nature but by the Spirit, if the Spirit of God lives in you"* (Romans 8:9 NIV).

Grace reveals the law of the spirit of life. The law of the spirit of life invites us to live in the present (Romans 8:2). If we believed we are forgiven and live from the realm of God's presence, we live from the law of the spirit of life.

Living from the new self places us in a devil free zone. The devil will have no entry points into our life, just as there were no entry points within Jesus, when we act with compassion and forgiveness. There will be no place for the devil to cause us to miss the mark of God's glory.

## Consider

- What are some of the ways that look harmless to you but lead to death?
- What does the word *glory* mean?
- How do our inner eyes help us to see?

*There is no-one righteous,*
*not even one;*
*there is no-one,*
*who understands,*
*no-one*
*who seeks God.*

(Romans 3:10-11 NIV)

# Twenty Four

# The Power of Influence

God desires his brilliant light
to shine through
us
into our circumstances
and
reveal his glory
in
our daily lives.

$W$e are made to leave impressions of God wherever we go, but because we do not understand our worth, we often leave the mark of sin. There are five main reasons why we find it hard to live out of the new self. We:

- fail to understand the nature of sin
- can't let go the past
- have a sense of worthlessness
- haven't got a vision of how God sees us.
- haven't been empowered to prosper.

## Sin

The Greek word for *sin* is *hamartia* and means missing the mark.[63] The Bible is clear that we have all missed the mark of God's glory (Romans 3:23). But what is this mark? Is it a stain or is it something altogether different?

The Greek word for *mark* is *charagma* and denotes a stamp or impress."[64] Imagine impressing your fingers in ink and pressing them all over the pages in your book. The exact marks of your fingerprints would be seen. We are designed to be the fingerprints of God. When we are filled with his Spirit, we will leave impressions of his love and grace as an aroma to those around us. Do we make an impression that leaves people feeling loved and appreciated or are we scribbling graffiti over their lives?

Although God has put eternity in our hearts not everyone desires to seek God. As a result we have become slaves to our selfish ways. We sin when we fail to allow God to influence our thoughts and actions. Such a failure opens us up further to our own devices and etches a deeper selfish attitude into our lifestyles.

Sin is the result of self-focus. Often we sin because we have reacted to a person who has marred our identity as one who is loved, valued or significant. When the enemy imprints an evil

or ugly image into our identity often we react with attitudes of "...
*hatred, discord, jealousy, fits of rage, selfish ambition, dissensions,
factions and envy, drunkenness, orgies and the like*" (Galatians
5:20-21 NIV). Suppose you hurt me and in response I rejected you.
Closing my heart to you is the first step to sinning. But suppose I
sought God and he gave me his opinion of you. What if he told me
of your unending worth? What if he told me that he is beholding
your face day and night and that he is always thinking about you?
Wouldn't that melt some of my hardened heart and bring me closer
to you? Of course it would. With that love in my heart I would have
no malice towards you.

> *Live freely, animated and motivated by God's spirit. Then
> you won't feel the compulsion of selfishness. For there is a
> root of sinful self-interest in us that is at odds with a free
> spirit, just as a free spirit is incompatible with selfishness.
> These two ways of life are antithetical, so that you cannot
> live at times one way and at times another way according
> to how you feel on any given day.*[65]

The Holy Spirit is always nudging and pointing us in the
right direction. We sin when we ignore these promptings. If we
seek God concerning our reactions we will be able to live without
hate in our hearts. We would live in an atmosphere of love for
others. Such will be the effect of the influence God would have on
us.

## *Looking back*

Those who succeed in the Christian life are those who, after
experiencing a trauma, pick themselves up and brush themselves
off and move forward. The way forward is to look ahead, not back.
Looking back keeps our focus fixed on ourselves. Throughout

this book we have been contemplating situations that have caused shame and reproach. If we find that we are always looking back to these times, the very image of what hurt us can become to us an idol that we find hard to erase from our mind. Instead of focusing on God and absorbing his peace, we hold the image of the past up in our mind. This particularly happens when a trauma has reshaped the way we see ourselves. We can't move forward while embracing situations that have caused a negative self-image. Looking back keeps us in bondage.

We can be set free from every false image that man has placed inside us by asking God for the truth. This truth can destroy all the false images that have kept us captive (2 Corinthians 10:5). It is only as we remove that false picture of ourselves will we be able to move forward. As we destroy the impact of our past we are then able to reach into the future. Embracing our God-given identity gives us the chance to discover the new thing that God is doing in our lives. *"Forget the former things; do not dwell on the past. See I am doing a new thing!"* (Isaiah 43: 18-19 NIV). God is doing something new. He encourages us to forget the past and embrace the future. *"You will forget the shame of your youth and remember no more the reproach of your widowhood"* (Isaiah 54:4 NIV).

## *Worthlessness*

Do you always think about yourself? Are you always on your mind? If we are always looking at ourselves we will live from the realm of our old self. Thinking about ourselves can intensify our sense of worthlessness. *"Focusing on the self is the opposite of focusing on God. Anyone completely absorbed with self ignores God and ends up thinking more about self than God."* [66] Hannah Hurnard discovered that thinking about herself made her daydream. When she had been hurt in real life, she escaped her pain by imagining that her circumstances were different to those currently making her upset. She imagined that instead of being rejected she was appreciated and known as being a gracious, charming gifted yet humble heroine. She saw day dreaming as an act of "burning incense … enthroning self in the centre of the stage of the imagination" However, almost invariably she noticed that after a time of day dreaming she was completely miserable and irritable. [67] We live defeated lives when are always thinking about ourselves.

Self-absorption and worthlessness are closely connected. Worthlessness prevents us realising our value and becomes an invisible film hiding a myriad of unmet needs to be loved and affirmed. The most powerful way we can care for our heart is to feed it with truth. The law of sowing and reaping is a law that can't be changed or overridden (Galatians 6:7-8). If we sow negative thoughts into our heart we will reap a bad self-image. If, on the other hand, we sow positive statements into our heart we will reap the identity that God has of us. Not only that, but we will find that the film over our hearts preventing us seeing our worth will be removed.

> *We can be set free from every false image that man has placed inside us by asking God for the truth.*

Many years ago I had a very poor self-image. I could not imagine that I was precious to God. So in resolve to rectify the problem I asked God to bring to my attention Bible verses that spoke of how he saw me. Each day, for about a year, I spoke those verses over my life. At first it appeared nothing changed. But eventually God opened up to me all that I had prophesied over my life. I was transformed through the Word of God.

# The power of wisdom

Jesus came to shine light into the darkness of our understanding of who we are. God's truth becomes a lamp that will guide us as we trek through a dark, negative world. *"People who sat in darkness have seen a great light. And upon those who sat in the region and shadow of death light has dawned"* (Matthew 4:16 NKJV). The wisdom that God gives becomes a light that helps us understand how he sees us (Psalm 43:3).

> *We can ask God for wisdom as to which part of our identity is being threatened.*

Since the tongue is guided by the heart it can rule the whole body. If your speech is negative perhaps consider that you may have an important piece of your identity missing. Our identity is made up of significance, belonging and personal value. If any one of these is threatened, we will defend ourselves.

We can ask God for wisdom as to which part of our identity is being threatened. If you are wise, says Solomon, *"your wisdom will reward you"* (Proverbs 9:12 NIV). His wisdom will compensate for all the damage the enemy has caused. God will pay us back by comforting us with his words of truth.

*If any of you lacks wisdom, he should ask God, who gives generously to all without finding fault, and it will be given to him. But when he asks, he must believe and not doubt, because he who doubts is like a wave of the sea, blown and tossed about by the wind. That man should not think he will receive anything from the Lord; he is a double-minded man, unstable in all he does.* (James 1:5-8 NIV)

What does wisdom look like? *"The wisdom that comes from heaven is first pure; then peace loving, considerate, submissive, full of mercy and good fruit, impartial and sincere"* (James 3:17). God does not tire of giving us wisdom. It is available to us day and night. When God speaks to us he creates peace in our hearts by redefining us according to his likeness. You will never hear God say that you are a loser and that there is no hope for you. He will lift you above your low level thinking and give you a new way of thinking. *"I have put my words in your mouth and covered you with the shadow of my hand"* (Isaiah 51:16 NIV).

When I was very young I was given an identity of being angry, but after searching, as if looking for a precious diamond, I found my treasure hidden in the still small voice of God. He both surprised and delighted me when I heard him say that "great gentleness" would surround my life. Those words became the vision for lasting change. Not only did God allow me to see gentleness, he also allowed me to see other aspects of his character that he had placed within me. I saw courage not fear, rest not striving, love not resentment, self-acceptance not rejection. This is not a matter of "blab it and grab it," but is based on the eternal vision given from God. God's vision concerning our identity gives us ability to see what others can't see. We should then allow the vision to penetrate our spirit and imagination.

Much of our future is determined by how we see ourselves. When leading a study group I taught the necessity of protecting our image to a group of young people. One member of the group, Dale, found it really hard to escape the pressures his peers were placing on him. Each week we would seek God concerning how he saw each of us. Dale would save each of these messages to his mobile phone and during the week would scroll through and allow these words to impact his response to situations he faced. Over the ensuring months I noted a dramatic change; his prophetic insight and inner peace increased and finally he was able to move forward in the call to witness to the students at his university. The vision Dale gained of his identity changed his life as he began to live out the image God had of him.

Receiving wisdom imparts vision and enables us to see ourselves the way God sees us. The result of seeking wisdom empowers us to deflect evil. This enables us to discover our true identity and motivates us to live a life of good behaviour (Proverbs 16:6). God's wisdom becomes a shield protecting our heart from all evil.

It is vital we believe God's vision of us because, "*If you do not stand firm in your faith, you will not stand at all*" (Isaiah 7:9 NIV). Applying the truth of who we are enables us to reflect love and faith during times of difficulty. By walking in the opposite spirit to how we are being treated allows God to chisel into our character an image that looks just like him. In the middle of a conflict, simply stop and choose to agree with what God says about you! We have been give power to defeat this evil world. We don't have to listen to its message. We can rise up in faith and destroy its voice.

Remaining pure and uncomplicated in the way we see ourselves enables us to develop an overcoming attitude. "*For everyone born of God overcomes the world.*" (1 John 5:4 NIV) Do you want to have good judgement so you can as far as possible live in peace with everyone? (Romans 12:18) Then seek wisdom from above.

## *Power of blessing*

Often we sin because we have never been recognised as having worth to succeed. Children receive their identity from significant people. When a parent speaks into a child, telling them who they really are, that child is then empowered to succeed. When Jacob called his sons to impart destiny into their lives before he died, he said this to Judah:

> *Judah, your brothers will praise you,*
> *You will grasp your enemies by the neck*
> *All your relatives will bow before you.*
> (Genesis 49:8-10 NLT)

But suppose a child has never received a blessing from his father. Suppose he has only received disapproval. Some kids have grown up being told they are good for nothing, or their life isn't worth living. Can these kids be empowered to live successfully?

The word *blessed* means to *cause to prosper.*[68] Perhaps we have had no one to bless us. This does not disqualify us. At the very core of our identity we are children who are chosen and loved by our heavenly Father. God asks that we turn our eyes from our family whom we love and receive from him, *"Forget your people and the house of your father. The king is enthralled in your beauty"* (Psalm 45:10-11 NIV).

My friend loved her family deeply. Since they had never experienced God's love she began to pray for them but saw little results. Every day for a number of years she had warred for them, but now had become tired in the fight. She came to me one afternoon and accepted my offer to stand with her in the battle. As we prayed God gave me a picture of her youngest daughter becoming a warrior princess. My friend began to use this image as a weapon of war against the enemy. As she smashed, by prayer, the distorted mirror she began to see a significant breakthrough in her daughter's life. This was only the beginning. God showed me her eldest daughter was a precious jewel in God's sight. Her husband was destined to rise up as a warrior; by wielding his sword he would destroy the darkness in people's lives. My friend had never seen how God viewed her family and this enabled her to fight for them with new zeal, believing that God wanted to restore to them their true image.

Throughout Scripture we see the Father placing his hand of blessing on our heads too. Such blessing lessens our fixation with this world. Receiving the Father's blessing frees us from seeking the opinion of man. When we truly know who we are the things that we had previously depended on to reveal our identity, all of a sudden, become desperately inadequate.

> *The LORD bless you and keep you;*
> *the LORD make His face shine upon you*
> *and be gracious to you;*
> *the LORD turn His face toward you*
> *and give you peace.*
> (Numbers 6:24-26 NIV)

*"As for God, his way is perfect,"* assures the psalmist (Psalm 18:30 NIV). God lacks nothing. When we mirror him, we too will not lack any good thing. Walking in our true identity provides a safe refuge, a strong tower and a mighty protection in the battles of life. Allow God to shape his characteristics into your identity. When our character is transformed into his image we won't need affluence, beauty or brains to define us. Free from the tyranny of things we will become comfortable with our eternal identity as we prepare to shine like stars in the age to come. We will live:

- free from the heavy weights of pleasing people
- courageously as we dodge damaging missiles of offence
- confidently liberated from the message trouble scribbles
- escaping the intimidation of negativity.

Our wholeness depends on how much of our spiritual DNA affects the way we live. *"But what happens when we live God's way? He brings gifts into our lives, much the same way that fruit appears in an orchard – things like affection for others, exuberance about life, serenity. We develop willingness to stick with things, a sense of compassion in the heart, and a conviction that a basic holiness permeates things and people.*"[69] When we know who we are we will want to spend our lives helping people to know who they are.

Jesus' body shone with a brilliant light as he was glorified before Peter. The brilliant light resident within Jesus penetrated outwards to the extent that his whole body shone (Matthew 17:1-2). As we embrace our true self, who is our new self, our transformation will begin to appear. God's light within us will similarly cause others to squint. We will inwardly be transformed in the same way that Jesus was outwardly transfigured before Peter on the mountain. God desires something of his brilliant light to penetrate through us into our circumstances and reveal his glory in our daily lives.

## Consider

- What are the five ways that prevent us from living from the new self?
- Do you find it hard to let go of the past?
- Have you experienced the blessing of God?
- Do you understand your worth?

# Section Three

Many, who are unaware of God's desire to be close, ask questions such as:

- *"Does God love me?"*
- *"Does God accept me unconditionally?"*
- *"Does he hear me when I pray to him?"*
- *"Is he close to me or far away?"*
- *"What is God's will for my life?"*
- *"Does he have good plans for me?"*
- *"Can I trust him?"*
- *"Why does God allow the enemy to attack me?"*

Moreover, many of us have not found adequate answers to these questions. For this reason we languish in our Christian lives. Progress is only possible when we know that God is close and that he has good plans for us. Knowing we are loved, hearing his voice and trusting his character enable us to become the reflectors we are designed to be.

In this section of the book, we are going to consider how our misconceptions about God can reflect back to us a distorted image of ourselves.

As you read ask the Holy Spirit to shine his torchlight into your heart and reveal to you how you really see God. Then ask him to give you a clearer perception of the God you were designed to reflect.

*His purpose in all of this was that the nations*
*should seek after God and*
*perhaps feel their way towards him*
*and find him - though he is not*
*far from any one of us.*

*For in him we live and move*
*and exist. As one your own poets says,*
*'we are his offspring'.*
*And since this is true, we shouldn't think of God*
*as an idol designed by craftsman*
*from gold or silver or stone.*

*God overlooked peoples'*
*former ignorance about these things,*
*but now he commands everyone everywhere*
*to turn away from their idols*
*and turn to him.*
(Acts 17:27-30 NLT)

# Twenty Five

# Blurred Vision

If our focus isn't zoomed in on God,
but rather is zoomed in on man,
we will see a blurred vision.

*You thought I was altogether like you.*
(Psalm 50:21 NKJV)

# Ensnared

*M*any Christians misunderstand the true heart of God. This is what God says to us,

> *But let him who boasts boast about this;*
> *that he understands and knows me,*
> *that I am the Lord, who exercises kindness,*
> *justice and righteousness on earth,*
> *for in these I delight.*
> (Jeremiah 9: 24 NIV)

The way we view God affects both the way we see ourselves and the way we treat others. We understand with our intellect that God is all-knowing, all-powerful and is present everywhere. He far surpasses our understanding and is exalted in power (Job 36:22). His dominion is an everlasting dominion (Daniel 4:34). He is the first and the last, the start and the finish and besides him there is no God (Isaiah 44:6). Yet we can live believing God has no power and that our situations are bigger than him.

We all have certain pictures or concepts of God in our mind's eye. If these pictures are faulty we will not be able to receive God's goodness. When people who have never met God tell us what he is like, more often than not, our picture of him will become distorted. At my conversion God revealed himself to me as someone who was passionately caring and extremely loving. Yet I was told by someone, whom I deeply respected, that God was cruel. I imagined God to be a god of punishment. This belief was not in my mind (I knew him to be a God of love) but became a fear in my imagination. Looking back I can't believe that I ate the bait when God had already allowed me to experience his deep love and approval.

The words, "God is cruel" created an inherent flaw in my

perception of him. Even though God had revealed himself to me with clear defining lines of love and grace, I found it hard to be close, I became distant and indifferent towards him. In my heart, I became afraid of God. That's when I decided to control my own life and keep God at a safe distance. Because I disliked the image I had of God I disliked myself.

God notices when we no longer trust him and it concerns him. Trust in man is a snare (Proverbs 29:25). The enemy of our image lies in wait to ambush us with a surprise attack. *Pagis* is the Greek word for *snare* and literally means "a trap."[70] When we believe people instead of God the trap snaps and we become focused on man's opinion. Our faith is robbed and we become unbelieving and unresponsive to God. Hebrews 3:12 says, *"See to it, brothers, that none of you has a sinful, unbelieving heart that turns away from the living God."*

> *The way we view God affects both the way we see ourselves and the way we treat others.*

We set ourselves up to be trapped into believing a wrong view of God when we don't take the time to find out first hand what he is like. We can't move forward when we only trust people to tell us who God is. For instance, if our view of God has only come from the male role models that we had as children, and others who falsely represented him, our concepts of him will be false. My dad, as a child, received floggings from his mum for not reading his Bible. He came away believing God was harsh and cruel.

Because men and women are often placed in positions of authority we tend to connect man's behaviour with God's nature. In making this connection between man and God, we become ensnared into believing a distorted view of God; rather than maintaining a view of a Father who is perfect. There are no inherent flaws, shades of darkness or shadows within God. He is pure unadulterated light (James 1:17). Yet, as long as we persist in equating God with man, the enemy will slander God's character in our minds on a daily basis.

Is God known or unknown to you? Is he close to you, or standing aloof watching you from a distance? The answer to this question is vital to understanding your worth. If God is distant or unknown, we will never be able to mirror his image properly. We are designed to reflect to the world a perfect image of God. Yet, if we see God as a god of punishment, we will reflect that perception by punishing others. If we believe that he is distant and indifferent, we will not spend time with him. If we believe that he is stingy, we will not be generous. If you see God as someone ready to pounce on you the moment you make a mistake, you will see your worth only in terms of your performance and judge others by the same standard. God knows that if we see him as being harsh, we will begin to see others and ourselves accordingly. If we believe God is tempting us, we will not come to him for understanding and forgiveness. If we believe God will hurt us or leave us, we will hold him at arm's length.

> *God is a mirror into which we can look and see our own reflection.*

If, however, we see God as the Father of light we will want to walk away from the shadows of sin so we can reflect that brilliant, pure light. If we see God as holy, we will reflect that image by purifying our thought life. If we see him as a God of grace, we will accept others unconditionally. When we see God as one who is capable, we will have confidence in him at all times. When we see God as someone who keeps his promises, we will also want to keep our promises.

# A Mirror to God's image

We are made to mirror God's likeness. When we take the time to find out for ourselves what he is really like we will be better able to clearly reflect him. Built within each one of us is a 'mirror' that automatically transposes our perception of God onto our attitudes in life. Have you kept God at a distance because you have glanced into the flawed images that other people have of him? Has the opinion of man shaped your view of God? If so, you will follow a god who is made in the image of people. God shares his nature with us so that others are able to see clearly what he is like. God gave us feelings, a mind to think with, the ability to achieve and communicate with each other, because he is able to feel, think, achieve, and communicate. We are able to choose and create because he also makes choices and creates. To be able to think like Jesus ensures that we reflect to the world the person we were created to be. We can truly experience the best life possible, free from bondage and fear, when we have a deep clear view of God.

God is a mirror into which we can look and see our own reflection. The more we look to God the more special we will feel. As we look to God we will become aware that we are made to reflect someone much bigger than ourselves. God does not wear masks; he is who he reveals himself to be. He longs that we become just like him.

## Consider

- Has there been a wrong perception of God etched deep within your heart?
- What feelings do you have about God?
- How are we made to be like God?

*So leave the corruption and compromise;*
*Leave it for good, says God.*
*Don't link up with those who pollute you*
*I want you all for myself.*[71]

# Twenty Six

# Rivals to Our True Image

*Don't copy the behaviour*
*and customs of the world,*
*but let God transform you into*
*a new person by changing*
*the way you think - then you will learn*
*to know God's will for you,*
*which is good and pleasing and perfect.*
(Romans 12:2 NLT)

# The world is a battlefield

*W*hen our view of God is distorted we will either totally ignore him or we will strive to please him. If we choose to ignore God then something else will become a god to us. We are made to relate to a higher being, but if we can't find something big enough we will become our own god. Self-actualisation is the god of our age. We believe the subtle yet dangerous lie that we are masters of our destinies and that we are the sole controllers of our lives.

Eternity has been placed within our hearts. To satisfy our longing for the eternal, God has shaped a vacuum within out heart that only Jesus can fill (Ecclesiastes 3:11). We all sense this vacuum, but not knowing why it is there, we fill it with things of the world.

*Since losing connection with God at the fall we are forever seeking to be reconnected.*

The shopping malls are geared not only to satisfy desire but to create it. Provocative clothing, scrumptious food and engaging entertainment feed our physical appetites. The world system feeds the appetites and desires that oppose God.

Our affections and desires are constantly under siege. The supernatural powers of both good and evil wage war over our God-made image. Our hearts and minds are the battlefield in which this war is being waged. Satan controls our carnal passions by convincing us that we always are in need of more than we have. The more he can get us to want, the greater advantage he has in winning the war over our hearts. God desires that we live blessed lives. He empowers us to prosper in everything we do. Yet we become confused when we pursue wealth and human love to prove to others, and even to ourselves, that God loves us. Do we measure a good relationship with God with what we have or don't have? If we do we could come close to chasing the gods of this world. If we insist that God has to bless us to prove his love we dance with the enemy. For many of us the enemy has his arms wrapped so tightly around us that we cannot move our hearts towards God.

## *The battle is brutal*

In our desperate search to find ourselves, has Christianity become a 'me-focused' religion? Has our faith in Jesus become all about us and how we compare with others? While there are valid aspects to furthering our success, we can forget that God primarily desires to shape us into his character.

It is entrenched in us to be connected to our spiritual heritage. Since losing connection with God at the fall we are forever seeking to be reconnected. Few of us understand this longing in our hearts, so we settle for the gods of the world to satisfy our need for the eternal. The gods of this world make us feel like we can live forever; they give us a false sense of security. In a million different ways they tell us that they have what it takes to reveal our worth. We pay a high price for the life they offer. We buy their cars and drink their wine. We end up nervous wrecks as we crank our credit cards up far beyond what we can afford, believing our empires will stand the test of time.

> *What good will it be for a man if he gains the whole*
> *world, yet forfeits his soul?*
> *Or what can we give in exchange for our soul?*
> (Matthew 16:26 NIV)

What do we really gain if we eventually achieve that perfect image the world has shaped for us, yet lose the true essence of who we are? Are the gods of this world able to open heaven's door? (Psalm 49:7-8). Remember we are eternal beings passing through this world to the next. Who can pay the price for our souls once we have passed from this life?

## The "God and" syndrome

The Westminster confession briefly sums up our purpose. "The chief end of man is to know God and enjoy him forever." Are you fulfilling your purpose? Do you know God and enjoy his friendship? Or do you look to the world to receive that love? When we choose other things, rather than God, to meet our deep need for the eternal, we are in fact saying that he isn't big enough to define our value.

> *You are cheating on God. If all you want is your own way, flirting with the world every chance you get, you end up enemies of God and his way. And do you suppose God doesn't care? The proverb has it that He is a fiercely jealous lover. And what He gives in love is far better than anything else you'll find.*[72]

We often go to God when we are in trouble, or if we need guidance or help in a test, but how many of us spend time with him for no reason at all? God desires our passionate devotion and longs for our company.

Many years ago God said to me, "My heart is burning with a gentle and yet fierce flame of love, gentle towards you and fierce towards all the predators that seek to destroy your life." There is a gentle flame of love burning in God's heart for all of us. Yet within that gentle flame of love, a jealous fire burns.

In the Old Testament, God

> God takes us to the wilderness to share his goodness with us and to become our own personal lover.

quarrels with his bride many times and complains that she has forgotten him (Jeremiah 2:32). Listen as God wistfully remembers the devotion of Israel,

> *I remember the devotion of your youth, how as a bride you loved me and followed me through the desert. ... What fault did your fathers find in me, that they strayed so far from me? ... I brought you into a fertile land to eat its fruit and rich produce, but you came and defiled my land and made my inheritance detestable.* (Jeremiah 2:2-7 NIV)

God is ablaze with passion that we draw close to him.

> *I myself said, "How gladly would I treat you like sons and give you a desirable land, the most beautiful inheritance of any nation, I thought you would call me 'Father' and not turn away from following me. But like a woman unfaithful to her husband, so you have been unfaithful to me, O house of Israel.* (Jeremiah 3:19 NIV)

God had a dilemma. He loved his people yet they did not respond to his love. In Hosea 11:8 God talks about giving his people up and handing them over to their lovers. But he relents and changes his mind.

> *My heart is changed within me;*
> *all my compassion is aroused.*
> *I will not carry out my fierce anger,*
> *nor will I turn and devastate Ephraim.*
> *For I am God, and not man -*
> *the Holy One among you.*
> *I will not come in wrath* (Hosea 11:8-9 NIV).

Can you hear something of the incredible tenderness deep within God's heart toward his people? He longs to woo us back into his arms. Rather than living for ourselves, God longs for us to have a single heart of devotion for him alone. God desires that we acknowledge that it is his extravagant heart that becomes the source of every good and perfect gift. Unless we deny all human securities, even to the point of denying our own agendas, we cannot fully appreciate the extent of his love for us (Luke 14:26). This does not mean we shut people out of our lives, or refuse to live by acceptable cultural standards, but it is a refusal to trust or depend on anyone or anything except God to tell us the deepest message about our worth.

## *Focus redirected*

God is jealous, especially when other lovers seduce us into following their ideologies. Because God is the only one who can give us a true and lasting sense of importance he desires to become our only source of identity. With a passion to be one in heart and spirit with us, God leads us away from our troubles and lures us into the desert.

> *Therefore I am now going to allure her;*
> *I will lead her into the desert and*
> *speak tenderly to her.*
> *There I will give her back her vineyards,*
> *and I will make the Valley of Achor*
> *a door of hope.*
> (Hosea 2:14-15 NIV)

Metaphorically the desert is known as a place of trouble. When we have lost sight of God we say that we are going "through a wilderness experience." Jesus knew the wilderness to be a place of testing. The Israelites knew it as a place of wanderings. But the wilderness, even though it may be initiated through trouble and testing, becomes a place of renewal and refreshment - a honeymoon with God. Contact with Jesus, seeing him face to face, will restore to us our true image.

## Honesty before God

We cannot see God if we aren't looking at him. God wants us to adjust the focus of our thoughts so we can see him. With our thoughts fixed on God he will gently speak to us and draw us close to himself. He allures each one of us with his tender words and soft overtures to a place where there is no one in our hearts but him. God desires that he becomes our own personal lover. He guides us into the wilderness so we can be as we originally were: naked before him. Nakedness is simply openness and vulnerability, a place where we are totally honest. Here we find out what motivates us and what particular things give us our significance. God takes us through the desert to reveal all the areas in our lives where we have in the past allowed people and things to define our worth. Very few of us will want to go to a place where the things that have been closest to our hearts are challenged.

> *We cannot see God if we aren't looking at him.*

The wilderness teaches us to depend on Jesus alone for our identity. The beloved in *Song of Songs* came up out of the wilderness leaning on her lover (Song of Songs 8:5). Leaning carries the idea of dependence. It is in the wilderness that we accept our identity as God sees it. We come out depending on his view of us and not the world's view. We come out of the wilderness responding with passion and devotion.

*Set me as a seal upon your heart,*
*as a seal upon your arm;*
*for love is as strong as death.*
(Song of Songs 8:6 NKJV)

Receiving God's goodness allows us to see what we really look like. The time that we spend with Jesus in our personal wilderness becomes a doorway of hope which brings us to a place where God will have no rivals to our affections.

God takes us to the wilderness to:

- reveal his true character
- reveal his love
- reveal his face
- discard the distractions in our lives
- speak to us
- shine his light onto our image.

When God's presence becomes our focus the world will not distract us and we will then be able to reflect our true light as an unstoppable force against the kingdom of darkness.

## *Consider*

- Have the gods of this world made you feel like you can live forever?
- Have they given you a false sense of security?
- Explain how our hearts become the battlefield in which the supernatural powers of both good and evil wage war over our God-made image.
- Have you allowed God to allure you into the desert?

# Twenty Seven

# Resilience before God

*Are you tired?*
*Worn out?*
*Burned out on religion?*
*Come to me. Get away with me*
*and you'll recover your life.*
*I'll show you how to take a rest.*
*Walk with me and work with me*
*- watch how I do it.*
*Learn the unforced rhythms of grace.*
*I won't lay anything heavy*
*or ill fitting on you.*
*Keep company with me,*
*and you'll learn to live*
*freely and lightly.* [73]

*S*alvation is an eternal gift that cannot be earned. Somehow very early in our Christian experience we pick up the message that we have to keep the scoreboard even. Being accepted is no longer a gift to be enjoyed but becomes a wage to be earned. When I first came to the desert I was physically and spiritually worn out. I had given my life to Jesus in my mid-teens but became exhausted trying to please him. Even though I enjoyed various levels of success in ministry I lacked both power and passion.

Most of us remember the incredible sense of rest that we experienced when we first believed in Jesus. Many of the burdens that we were carrying disappeared. We entered a rest called the *Sabbath rest*. On conversion we experienced an acceptance from God that we didn't earn. It is no different now. We will never earn God's acceptance. We must accept his love knowing that it can't be taken from us.

## A life of rest

When we are convinced that God is good and that he has on open heart toward us we can enter an amazing rest whereby we no longer strive. As we rest we are more able to receive his grace (Hebrews 4:10-11). Every day as I look up and connect with God's love his attitude towards me changes me.

> *Only crazy people would think they could complete by their own efforts what was begun by God. If you weren't smart enough or strong enough to begin it how do you suppose you can perfect it? Does the God, who lavishly provides you with his own presence, His Holy Spirit, working things in your lives you could never do for yourselves. Does he do these things because of your strenuous moral striving or because you trust him to do them in you?*[74]

Entering God's rest enables us to live confidently knowing that he has saved us from eternal punishment and will continue to save us from our own inadequacies and shortcomings. It took God many years to teach me that walking in rest was a simple matter of believing that we are totally acceptable. Jesus saved us without any effort on our part; he now wants to live his life through us with that same amount of ease.

God spoke into my heart many years ago concerning this. He said, "Man sees activity as serving me. I see love and rest, mixed with trust that I will indeed lead you, as true service. My child, I know that you have heard my call, and yet, in hearing, is to a different beat from those who feverishly try to please me. Rest in the knowledge that I am leading you into my plans and purposes and that right now, as you wait on me to hear me speaking, you are fulfilling my will for your life."

> *Jesus saved us without any effort on our part; he now wants to live his life through us with that same amount of ease.*

## *Stop impressing me!*

While in the Solomon Islands I remember clearly hearing God speak to me. He said, "Stop trying to impress me!" These words changed the entire direction of my life. For the remainder of the year I took one word at a time very slowly until I actually understood what it meant.

First I stopped. I stopped all my frantic endeavours and I just waited in his presence. I actually learnt to feel his presence. I did not talk to God; I just became aware that he was with me. I learnt to be still. I sat in that stillness and waited.

Then I stopped trying. I became aware that I had been striving. I stopped trying to be everything to everyone. I stopped trying to have all the answers and to be more than I actually was. I stopped pretending and the yokes began to feel a lot lighter.

Then I asked God how I was trying to impress him. It was in the secret place that God showed me that I thought I had a lot of faith when I prayed, but actually I had a lot of fear. I tried to impress him with my dedication, but really I had misgivings about the service that he required of me. I tried to impress God with my unending love, but I had a lot of resentment about how he allowed people to treat me. I was being unreal, I was pretending.

> *As our picture of God becomes clearer, our desire to spend time with him will increase.*

I was trying to impress God so that he would like me. My life changed forever when he showed me that I didn't ever have to impress him. He loved me before I was born. He knew about me light years ago and liked me then! He chose me to belong to him before the foundation of the world (Ephesians 1:4). God loved me while he was making me in the secret place of his heart. I will never be ever able to do anything for God that will cause him to love me more than he does at this moment. God is easy to please. His attitude towards us is always encouraging and affirming; he is intensely gentle.

God creates a space in our hearts for himself, but he is a gentleman and will not barge his way in. He knows we need convincing that we are loved. It is only as we remove the negative pictures that we have in our minds will we be able to relax. He is at peace with us. He wants to hold us close so we can hear him saying that we are very precious. He wants to surprise us with his gentleness.

This new found acceptance may take a while to get used to. I remember when I first started meeting God I was not used to pure selfless love. As I became aware that God was offering me his heart, initially I held back, withdrawing myself. I sensed that God was aware of what was happening. He came to me many times, but I would not, (dare I say, I could not) open my heart to him. Finally, after weeks of running from him, his extravagant love caught up with me. I found myself being vulnerable. I told him that I was afraid that if I fully opened my heart to him, he would turn and close his heart to me. He was able to convince me that he could be trusted and that he would never do that ... EVER! That was many years ago now, and since then I have enjoyed many years of intimacy with him.

> *"I'll live in them, move into them;*
> *I'll be their God and they'll be my people.*
> *... I'll be a Father to you;*
> *You'll be sons and daughters to me."*[75]

Jesus held a constant gaze towards the Father. He rested in the Father's acceptance and clearly reflected him to the world (John 5:19). As we train our eyes to see what the Father is doing we will cease striving from our own need to make everything happen and, we too, will enter amazing rest. As our picture of God becomes clearer, our desire to spend time with him will increase. We will then hear him encourage us with sweet words of acceptance. God's love will easily flow out of us into a lost and broken world.

You are forever acceptable to God. When you discover this truth, you will wake up tomorrow knowing that you do not have to impress either man or God, you will enter into an incredible rest.

# Consider

- When we expect God to accept us because of what we do for him we will develop a deep insecurity. How will this insecurity affect our lives?
- How does resting in God enable us to receive his grace?
- Describe God's rest.

# Twenty Eight

# Mirror of Destiny

*No eye has seen,*
*no ear has heard,*
*no mind has conceived*
*what God has prepared for*
*those who love Him - but God*
*has revealed it to us by His Spirit.*
(1 Corinthians 2:9 NIV)

*Before I formed you in the womb I knew you,*
*Before you were born I set you apart;*
*I appointed you as a prophet to the nations.*
(Jeremiah 1: 5 NIV)

*T*here has been an assignment against our identity. Rather than destroying our identity with hurtful words or images of being unrighteous, the enemy highjacks it by taking us into a different direction than what God had originally designed. Our giftings are designed to reveal God's talents, but if we focus on our achievements, his talents become blurred into the sea of our self-absorption.

When I hear a beautiful voice, I think that God's voice must be awe inspiring. When I admire an artist, a poet, a writer, a builder, an accountant, a musician, a florist, a homemaker, I do so because all of these gifted people display the talents that are within God.

God shares his talents within us. God knew what part of himself he planned to share with us before he made us. Just as houses are built to specified plans, so also God has a plan for our lives. We are all given talents that express something of God's creative abilities. Before we were born God drew up our blueprint detailing the ways in which we would be able to express the talents he put within us.

To find our purpose we need to discover our passion. This does not mean we pursue our sensual passions. God has placed within each of us various aspects of himself that can bring heaven to earth. As we seek God concerning the destiny that he has put within us, he will speak from the perspective of these amazing plans, and not merely from where we are right now. We should not be surprised if he says something which seems to be outside the realm of our possibility.

Everyone needs a reason to live! In view of eternity bringing our true identity into 20/20 vision remains one of the main purposes of our lives. It is vital that we understand who we are if God is going to use us in any significant way.

## The problem

God does not give us a destiny so that we can make a name for ourselves. Our talents are to make God's name known. It is essential that we do not allow our talents to give us an identity that God never intended for us to have. Some of us are tempted to fall at the feet of our destiny and worship it as if that is what gives us value.

> *Satan would like to high jack our talent so people will talk about us rather than God.*

Confidence in our natural abilities looks like this: I am important because I … (You fill in the blank). When we place our confidence in the things that give us our significance we place our confidence in the flesh. God wants us to place our confidence in him. Relying on our own strength prevents the Holy Spirit working through us. The same *dynamis* power working within Peter was enough to seep from his own shadow and bring healing to those who touched it (Acts 5:15). Paul was another who knew that he did not have to be competent in himself. Because he knew of the source of his power, he had confidence that he was in fact able to do all things through him who strengthened him. *"Not that we are competent in ourselves to claim anything for ourselves, but our competence comes from God"* (2 Corinthians 3:4 NIV). I too know through intimate experience that the power of his might will always support me (Philippians 3:3).

Satan would like to high jack our talent so people will talk about us rather than God. Satan tried to make a name for himself by what he did. He was the chief worshipper in heaven and he allowed that job to tell him something about himself, rather than allowing his gifting to exalt God.

Sometimes God is ready to use us before we are willing to be used. Such was the case with Jeremiah. When God felt it was time to make Jeremiah his mouth piece, Jeremiah replies, "*I am only a child*" (Jeremiah 1:6 NIV). God convinced Jeremiah to surrender his will and from there he was able to use him.

Others are willing to be used before their hearts are surrendered. Moses was such a man. He was passionate to see his people delivered from slavery, but his effort to achieve deliverance caused him to overstep his mark and flee. Although Moses sensed that God had big dreams for him, God had to dismantle everything that made him important before man. Moses knew that he was significant to God, but God went to great lengths to destroy the independent spirit in him.

## *Surrender*

Jacob wanted desperately to be somebody important. He was a schemer. He plotted and conspired ways to further his well-being. He strove to always come out on top. Every obstacle that life presented to him, he overcame in his natural strength. He was a smart cookie (he probably attended that self-help seminar that was in town last week). God had to strip Jacob of the strength that lay within his natural self. To do this he took Jacob through a painful process that made him realise that he had no strength within himself. That night as he wrestled with God under the stars his life was forever changed. He realised that God was stronger than he was. God's strength overpowered him (Genesis 32:22-32). He limped for the rest of his life.

When we become aware of the plans that God has for us we need to surrender them to God so that he can deal with all the hindrances that would prevent those plans being realised. If we grasp tightly, the dream itself could become like a rock that looks solid, but is in fact, easily crushed and able to slip through our fingers. With an open hand we need to be willing for God to take those dreams from us if he chooses. God has to topple all our idols of self-sufficiency before he can release us into the destiny that he has for us.

God organises our circumstances so that his plans for us are fulfilled. Initially these circumstances may prevent those plans being realised. These situations become a bridge over which we must cross. Sometimes the overpass may include being rejected and ridiculed by people who should appreciate us. Joseph, while journeying to a place where God was able to use him to save a nation, experienced rejection, accusation, oppression, and loneliness brought about by his own family. We cannot bypass the method that God uses if we want to be the person who can achieve his plans.

*Often God tests us to see if our gifting is more important to us than our relationship with him.*

Most of the things that define us are temporary and passing. Perhaps we have a ministry that gives us a sense of great worth. But think about it, at any moment, circumstances could change and the ministry could be taken from us. If losing our position before man would cause us to be despondent, then it is our position, rather than our relationship, that has become so crucial to our sense of worth. Often God tests us to see if our gifting has become more important to us than our relationship with him. God is more interested in the condition of our heart, and our relationship with him, than in what we can do for him. When our significance comes solely from being God's child nothing will be able to discourage us. When we understand that being God's loved, chosen child defines us, we will lessen our hold on trusting our own abilities and will relax with the destiny that God has for us.

Knowing that our gifting does not define us, allows us to concentrate on being children who possess God's character. When our character is strong, the dreams will then become to us as a solid rock that no one can take from us. God brings us to a place where we will rely on "*being strengthened with all power according to his glorious might so that you may have great endurance*" (Colossians 1:11 NIV).

> *Knowing that our gifting does not define us, allows us to concentrate on being children who possess God's character*

Our human strength is not equal to God's *dynamis* power. The secret to finding our strength is in connecting ourselves to God. God has within himself an unending source of strength. He does not grow weary, nor does he faint. To experience unending strength we need to set our gaze on God, wait in his presence and incline our hearts toward him. As we wait on God his strength will be infused into our being. God has enough strength within himself to work on behalf of every person in every situation. I have witnessed God's strength work on my behalf many times and I expect to see him come through in future situations.

As you spend time with God you will discover the plans that God has for you. God's indelible plans are positioned within your life waiting to be tapped. As you ask God about the gifting and talents he has placed within you allow yourself to go through the process of being shaped into the image God has of you.

## Consider

- How much do you look to others for approval?
- Why does God shape our character before he releases our destiny?
- Why is it important that we gain our identity from our relationship with God rather than what we do for him?

"God's love
will soften
the most unbelieving heart –
would soften
even
the hardest
of
hearts."[76]

## Twenty Nine

# The Perfect Mirror of God's Love

*I have loved you my people with an everlasting love*
*With unfailing love I have drawn you to myself.*
(Jeremiah 31:3 NIV).

*When we experience God's love*
*we experience God.*

God made us so that we could experience a love so great that it is unable to be measured. God's love is like the vast unexplored ocean; it can never be fully surveyed. This immeasurable love is seen in the way God treats us. God's love is free from all forms of abuse, neglect and mistreatment. God our Father is someone who is neither demanding nor indifferent. He is at all times gentle, patient and full of goodness. God is mighty in strength and understanding and he despises no-one. He gives justice to the oppressed (Job 36:5). He comforts and is full of compassion (Lamentations 3:22). He heals broken hearts (Psalm 147:3) and has copious amounts of kindness (Nehemiah 9:17). He makes our way perfect by giving us the strength and wisdom to make right decisions (Psalm 18:32). Jesus' love has no conditions. It is a gift. Nothing will ever be able to detach you from God's indestructible love.

Receiving God's love transforms our lives into conduits that are then able to carry his love. However, many of us have faulty connections to the power source. This happens because we take our eyes off God and focus on people, expecting them to love us the same way God does. Instead of receiving clear pictures of love from God, we receive inconsistent messages from people.

For instance, in one breath people love us but in the next they are angry and criticise us for not measuring up to their standards. The promised love is withdrawn. When human love disappoints us do we then subconsciously transfer this disappointment onto God? If we have been betrayed by people who won our trust, do we now fear that God will betray us? If you have been used and then thrown away, do you fear God will do the same? If we have been physically or emotionally abandoned, do we believe that God also will abandon us? These damaged perceptions create a wall between us and God; they prevent us understanding his love.

When we associate God's love with the faulty messages that we have received from people, it becomes easy then to question whether God really loves us. Instead of running into his love, we run from his love. The confusion this brings leaves us standing empty with a dangerously divided heart. Even though Jesus openly displayed his love for us at the cross many of us doubt his love. I lived most of the early part of my Christian life doubting God's love. Up until the time Jesus calmed the storm when I was in the Solomon Islands I secretly doubted his love. God stilling the raging storm on the sea was the beginning of him stilling the emotional storm in my heart. From that time onwards every time I faced a doubt concerning my identity, he would remind me to rest in his love. Jesus would often say to me,

> *Doubting that we are loved by God is one of the biggest obstacles preventing us reflecting his image.*

> *The Lord has taken away your punishment; He has turned back your enemy. The Lord, the King of Israel is with you; never again will you fear any harm. He will take great delight in you. The Lord your God is with you, He is mighty to save, He will take great delight in you, He will quiet you with His love. (Zephaniah 3:15, 17 NIV)*

Doubting that we are loved by God is one of the biggest obstacles preventing us reflecting his image. Nothing ultimately has power to destroy God's love for us; not even people. Therefore we need to repent from making wrong judgments about God's love. As we do this and look only to God, he will give us new imagery that will show us clearly what his love looks like. We can rise up,

243

challenge and overcome all the obstacles that make us doubt his love.

> *God is love, and all who live in love live in God and God lives in them. And as we live in God, our love grows more perfect. So we will not be afraid on the Day of Judgment, but we can face him with confidence because we are like Christ here in the world. Such love has no fear, because perfect love expels all fear. If we are afraid, it is for fear of punishment, and this shows we have not fully experienced his perfect love.* (1 John 4:17-20 TNLT)

God's love reveals our true worth, "*As the father has loved Me, so I have loved you. Abide in My love*" (John 15:9 NKJV). Knowing we are loved defines us as having immense worth and is vital to understanding our true eternal image.

## God's love is indestructible

God has a keen eye for beauty and he sees in you what he is looking for. His love is resolute. He doesn't tinker with our hearts; he desires to weave unbreakable threads of love into our hearts mending all our brokenness. Experiencing God's love empowers us to understand the immensity of our worth. As we open our hearts to God we will discover that he always believes the very best about us. No matter how much we doubt God's love his commitment to us will never fade. He keeps the vision of us receiving the full depth of his love before him day and night.

> *God has a keen eye for beauty and he sees in you what he is looking for.*

Our hearts are designed to experience an eternal exchange of love and yearning. Yet true heart to heart intimacy is found in disclosing to God our naked broken self. We need to open our hearts up to him in complete honesty. Knowing and being known by God, and still being loved by him, involves an emotional risk. It involves sharing our deepest selves with him. We are to remove all our pretence and bring our real selves to God. When we are assured that he won't turn his back on us, no matter how bad we might seem, we will then have confidence to let our guard down and become transparent. When we tell God our doubts, his reassurance allows the knowledge that we have about his love in our heads to be transferred into our hearts. God's Word can only become real when we believe it.

Do you understand the immensity of God's love for you? Paul prayed that our eyes would be opened to such an extent that we would understand the enormity of our calling. We need that love to become the greatest thing in our lives.

*That Christ might dwell in your hearts through faith and that you,*
*being rooted and established in love,*
*might have the power together with all the saints,*
*to grasp how wide and long and high and deep*
*is the love of Christ,*
*and to know this love that surpasses knowledge –*
*that you may be filled to the measure*
*of all the fullness of God.*
(Ephesians 3: 17-19 NIV)

## Nothing can erase God's love

Even if through our own choices, life has taken a wrong turn, we need to understand that our value is not diminished in God's sight.

You have great value. God surrounds you with his exquisite love. His love will shine light into our deepest darkness and will remove all that tarnishes our true likeness. Nothing in all creation will be able to separate you from his love. Because God loves you, he will never forget you.

> *Can a mother forget the infant at her breast, walk away from the baby she bore? But even if she forgot you – I'd never forget you, never. Look, I've written your names on the backs of my hands.*[77]

Faith is the only requirement needed to receive God's love. Colour, race or social status does not prevent us from receiving his love. God will not relent in his pursuit of our affection. He will keep revealing his love so that it redefines our moments. As the imprint of his love is sealed on our hearts we will easily express this love to others.

Even though God offers us his love and friendship he awaits our response. He has given us a will. The choice is ours as to whether we befriend God or not. Even though Jesus welcomes us into an intimate relationship, he does not close his heart to us when we fail to respond to his overtures. He knows our faltering steps to grasp a love beyond understanding. Tell him your doubts and fears and then listen to his assurance of eternal love for you. Jesus is returning for a pure and passionate people who love him and love others without reserve.

> *So let God work his will in you.*
> *Yell a loud no to the devil and*
> *watch him scamper. Say a quiet yes to God and he'll be there in no time. Quit dabbling in sin.*
> *Purify your inner life.*[78]

## Consider

- Doubting that we are loved prevents us knowing our worth. Why is this?
- How can damaged perceptions block our understanding of God's extravagant love?
- Do you feel loved by God?
- When can we let our guard down and become transparent with God?

"God waits to be wanted."[80]

# Thirty

# Oasis in the Desert

*Here's what I want you to do:*
*find a quiet place so you won't be tempted*
*to role play before God.*
*Just be there as simply and honestly as you can manage.*
*The focus will shift from you to God*
*and you will begin to sense his grace.*[79]

## How can I know God?

Deep within our hearts is our need to experience divine love. When we meet Jesus love is awakened in our spirit. It is this very awakening that Jesus becomes our first love. During the process of life many things come to steal our passion for the one who initially awoke love within us. When this passion is stolen the fire in our hearts dies down and we become lukewarm. Although we are still interested in God we stand at a distance.

Like a jilted lover, Jesus comes to us with a gentle rebuke. "*Yet I hold this against you: you have forsaken your first love*" (Revelations 2:4 NIV).

Remember, the desert is a place of openness. It is a place of becoming real with our feelings. "*Never hide your feelings from him.*"[81] Hiding our feelings prevent our true beauty and strength being discovered. We can hide our true feelings behind our pursuit of pleasure or addictive lifestyles. Some even hide while pursuing the frantic pace of church leadership. We can hide behind the veneer of doctrine, or a life principle or a particular set of rules or in frantic activity. The result is that we fail to come close. In the movie, *I am Sam*, Sam built an origami wall of paper believing that it would prevent Rita from finding him. Often our walls are only paper thin but God sees us hiding there.

Countless times I have found myself hiding my true feelings from God. Yet throughout my many attempts of playing hide and seek with God he continually revealed his desire to be close. On one occasion he gave me a vision that I was at the end of my life and I was drawn right into heaven where I heard Jesus say to me, "You wasted your life. You never knew just how much I loved you. You never let me be yours; you wanted to live your life for yourself. You did not want me to share your moments, your hurts, your discoveries and your passions. You shut me out of your heart, locked the door and put a bar across it that said, 'Do not enter'.

You never invited me into the rooms where you live. You assumed that you were not good enough for me. I now remain a stranger in your world. You were too busy doing my work to spend time with me. I want to be your friend and share myself with you."

God knows the language of our hearts and he is the only one who can reach in and reveal our true value. To both know God and enjoy him we need to be honest and tell God how we really feel. Just as gentle and open interaction everyday with our spouse is the key to good solid relationships so also God desires that we relate to him on a daily basis. This does not mean that we fax through our shopping list first thing in the morning and thank him for a great day at night. It means that we invite him to become intimately involved in our moments.

> *God does not want us to follow him from a distance.*

God wants our attention and longs for us to be real with him. We were made to enjoy a lasting, intimate and personal interchange with God every moment of every day. "God is a person, and in the deep of His mighty nature He thinks, wills, enjoys, feels, desires and suffers as any other may. In making Himself known to us He stays by the familiar pattern of personality. He communicates with us through avenues of our minds, our wills and our emotions."[82] God doesn't want to be one of our many mirrors that speak to us concerning our worth. He wants to be our only mirror. When he alone tells us who we are we will better understand our true identity.

Tozer says, "Before a man can seek God, God must first have sought the man … the impulse to pursue God originates with God."[83] We can be certain that our search for God will be rewarding (Jeremiah 29:13-14). As we search with our inner eyes at the same time God will be drawing us close to himself. God invites us into the wilderness to encounter him personally. God desires that we let all of our agendas go. He doesn't want us wasting our time proving ourselves to him.

One day, as the sand slipped through my fingers at the beach, God spoke to me and said, "Every grain is a thought I have about you." I looked along the expanse of the beach having never seen sand in this light before. His thoughts about us are not only precious they are also prolific (Psalm 139). Those same precious thoughts are kept within his heart waiting for that day when we are sick and tired of being harassed by doubts and fears concerning who we really are.

> *Even when standing in our well-constructed gutter of cynicism God remembers our worth.*

Even when standing in our well-constructed gutter of cynicism God remembers our worth. He doesn't wait for us to be perfect. Instead he wraps his arms around us when we stand in the icy winds of our own self-rejection. With those tender arms, he reaches down from heaven, picks us up and draws us close to himself. He kisses our life with everlasting love. He washes off the dust of false images and declares us righteous. *"See I have taken away your sin, and I will put rich garments on you"* (Zechariah 3: 4 NIV). His perfect image of us will melt all the icicles that have numbed our heart.

## God is with you

As we begin to feel our deep need of him, it is wonderful to know that whatever point we are at in life, Jesus is right there to rescue and save. Right now, God knows where you are and what you are feeling. He knows what you are doing and what you are thinking.

Whether you are thriving in a realm of love, faith and rest, or have made your bed in a pit of despair, God is with you. He desires to reveal his intimate love and presence.

*Let him kiss me with the kisses of his mouth – for your love is more delightful than wine. Pleasing is the fragrance of your perfumes; your name is like perfume poured out. No wonder the maidens love you! Take me away with you – let us hurry! Let the king bring me into his chambers.*
(Song of Songs 1:2- 4 NIV)

God calls us into relationship with him whereby we are able to experience a love more delightful than wine and sweeter than perfume. Jesus is *"radiant and ruddy, outstanding among ten thousand. His head is purest gold ... His mouth is sweetness itself, he is altogether lovely"* (Song of Songs 5:10-11, 16 NIV).

## *God's goodness is discovered in the secret place*

There is a place which the Bible calls the *"secret place"* (Psalm 27:5) where we can be completely transparent. Even while facing everyday issues of life his tenderness will melt off all the hard layers surrounding our hearts.

Jesus invites us to come away by ourselves to a quiet place in our hearts where we can receive rest for our souls. We can come to this place even in our busiest of days. It is not a physical place of solitude but a spiritual place where we encounter God. Rather than hiding from God within the shadows of our own self-doubt, we can come to God and hide in the shelter of his total acceptance. It is as we find our place under his wings that we will discover that he knows us at the very depth of our being.

253

# Storehouse of identity

I have discovered the secret place through lifting my inner eyes to God in prayer. Prayer is the attitude of faith that connects us to God. Jesus said, *"When you pray, go into your room, close the door and pray to your Father, who is in unseen"* (Matthew 6:6 NIV). As we shut the door to our circumstances and enter this place of intimate audience God enables us to understand our true spiritual identity.

> *The most important journey that we will ever take will be into the secret place.*

As we feel God drawing us we will run after him in passionate pursuit. The secret place brings us into a greater understanding of God's heart and will release his favour over our lives. As we sit in his presence we feel loved, accepted and encounter incredible intimacy. Our hearts will finally discover their true home. Each time we go into God's presence, his words will surprise and excite us. They will renew our sense of identity; lift us to new heights, expand our view and give us understanding of the depth of our worth. God is passionately eager to reveal to us our true selves.

# Amazing journey

The most important journey that we will ever take will be into the secret place. The air is exhilarating, the shorelines are endless and the views are breathtaking. The possibilities of being renewed are beyond our dreams. If you have not experienced this place it may sound to you obscure and elusive. The reality is that it is a place of extravagant freedom. The secret place is designed for you alone.

Nobody else can enter the place within God's heart that he has reserved just for you.

In the secret place you will discover how God sees you regardless of how you see yourself. It is full of material to revamp your lives, so that you will be truly happy. The secret place is a safe place. By fixing our eyes on Jesus we can go there at any time.

God is waiting for us and longs to meet us there. He is checking to see if we are on our way and his heart skips a beat with excitement when he sees us coming home. It is in this place that he patiently waits to enthral our hearts with truth about ourselves. As we look into the mirror of his heart we will see that we are made to be like him.

Entering the secret place is not at all difficult or complicated. Its path is not a maze of dead ends and brick walls. God does not tantalise us by offering us a relationship that he does not plan to fulfil. The door has been made wide open for us by Jesus, who powerfully pushed back every obstacle at the cross. By faith, believe that God is right there with you, look up into his face and walk right in. He is there, waiting for you.

## Consider

- What is the secret place?
- How can we go there?
- Is God a lover in pursuit of your affection?
- Does God have to take his place and wait for you?
- How close are you to God?

Come away to me your father
Draw near and talk of love
Come; tell me what I mean to you,
How you need your Father above.

Then quietly wait and listen,
There's much I want to say,
You're far too busy doing things,
Let go, child come away.

Do you realise that I'm waiting?
Do you know you're my delight?
Come away My child and talk with me,
You are precious in my sight.

Your words have said you love me,
Do you mean it, do you care?
Then stop and tell your Father so,
Come away – you know I'm there.

Joan Gooda

# Thirty One

# But I am so Busy

*But those who wait on the Lord*
*shall renew their strength:*
*they shall mount up with wings as eagles,*
*they shall run and not be weary,*
*they shall walk and not faint.*
(Isaiah 40:31 NKJV)

# The price of focus

*T*he Bible says, *"Be still and know that I am God"* (Psalm 46:10 NIV). One of the hardest things to do as the pace in life quickens is to be still.

The world demands that we march to its feverish drumbeat. The urgency in the air today insists we grab as much as we can to fill our God-shaped vacuum. In the midst of our busy lives many of us feel empty, devoid of any real purpose and meaning that will sustain us.

We are erroneously led to believe that a busy life is an abundant life. But instead of abundance, we become distracted as we fill our inner emptiness with the urgent. Living a life of distraction is responsible for much of our constant worry, inner tension and stress.

Martha was stressed. Luke records for us the scenario (Luke 10:38-42). The doorbell rang, Jesus was coming for dinner. Martha was frantic with the roast in the oven and the flowers on the table were not sitting right. Nevertheless, Mary did not seem to care. This frustrated Martha, who couldn't make up her mind whether she wanted to spend time with Jesus or finish cooking dinner. She was drawn in different directions; her outward circumstances were causing inward pressure. She was harassed with a divided heart!

Having a vision for eternity allows us to keep everything in perspective. Such a vision enables us to make a distinction between the urgent and the important. Mary was someone who had such a vision. She knew what was urgent, and what was important. With her eyes fixed on Jesus she soaked up his every word. In doing so she chose what she needed the most. Jesus commended her and promised that her encounters with him would not be taken from her.

Martha was in the fast lane when Jesus came to her house. *"Martha, you are troubled and worried about many things."* Sounds pretty familiar doesn't it? Sometimes we are unaware of the momentum we are gaining. We need to discover how to put the brakes on when we are going too fast in life. I remember being in the fast lane of ministry. It was exhilarating and I knew there was a small segment of my self-focused life that was being fed. People appreciated me and they told me so. In essence the "roast and the flowers" had distracted me. Yet I was dissatisfied! God's constant presence had been a big part of my life. But now busy with many other agendas, whenever I reached out for him, even though I would feel his presence, I had to rush away.

> *The secret to spending time with Jesus is simply having no agenda for him to fulfil.*

Is our momentum creating emptiness within our heart? Jesus cares about this emptiness more than we realise. We are but a vapour. Why is it that we busily look for an identity that gives us worth before people? Rather, if we look for our identity in the person of Jesus we will discover our true eternal value.

Are you too busy to fit God into your life? Busyness has become a way of life. There is too much to do and as the old saying goes, time waits for no man. Our mobile phones, emails and ipod demand immediate and constant attention. Modern technology not only steals our time but can also steal our hearts and affections away from God.

We are one heartbeat away from eternity. There we will spend the rest of our lives. Surely discovering who we are and where we will spend eternity is an important matter. In spending time with Jesus that day, in the midst of much criticism, Mary found the mirror that was able to reveal her true value.

# Slow down!

To discover our identity is to discover the reason for our existence. The Bible says that Jesus is our starting point for greatness and is our only hope to receiving God's goodness (Colossians 1:27).

When we first come into the secret place we will need to slow down. Everything within us may resist this but the results will be profound. Solitude is rare today. We are so rushed we have little idea of what is going on in our hearts. Our frantic pace is one of the main culprits creating instability.

## Distracted focus

Growing up, I remember my brother and sisters and I loved climbing. Many times we would climb our dad's ladder onto the roof of our house. There we could look down. Instead of seeing only what was in front of us, our vision was expanded. Our image is like that. When we desire the world to tell us who we are our view is limited and we become preoccupied with only what we see in front of us. When we look up and focus on Jesus our image is expanded and we get a better view of ourselves.

> *Having a vision for eternity allows us to keep everything in perspective*

We can sidestep instability by spending time with God. *"He who dwells in the secret place of the Most High shall remain stable and fixed under the shadow of the Almighty."*[84] Being still in God's presence is a very effective way of dealing with the stress of life. God himself becomes our constancy. The enemy of our souls knows this and he sabotages our time with God by placing before us a myriad of options. If we listen to his voice, these options will distract us. When I was a child

I'd love to go into a cathedral and absorb the silence that permeated the atmosphere. I would go in there, sit down and wonder what God was thinking. I wondered if he felt lonely when everyone went home. In my childlike thinking I thought that church was where God lived. Today I have come to realise that God lives in our hearts. In our rush, however, he is ignored. But when we spend time with Jesus his thoughts will become our thoughts, his desires will become our desires and his focus becomes our focus. Even though we remain separate individuals, becoming one in heart and spirit with him, enables his likeness to become more evident in our lives.

The secret to spending time with Jesus is simply having no agenda for him to fulfil. Spending time with God increases our expectation that he is with us. Being still in our emotions, quietening our hearts and believing that he is with us provides the right atmosphere in which we can draw close to God. Waiting on God intertwines our lives with his. As we become entwined with God he changes us into his image.

> *Yet the Lord longs to be gracious to you; he rises to show you compassion. For the Lord is a God of justice. Blessed are all who wait for him.*
> (Isaiah 30:18 NIV)

God has a fire in his heart. He desires that we catch that flame. Spending time with Jesus renews our mind and transforms our lives. If we live before God in the secret place, desiring only to please him, we will tap into the important agenda for our lives.

The kingdom of heaven belongs to those who hunger for God enables them to inherit everything (Matthew 5:3&6). Being aware of our spiritual need has nothing to do with what we own. We don't have to be poor to be *poor in spirit*. In fact those who know their need of God may be millionaires or on top of the corporate world, but the affluence is around them and not in them. There are many wealthy people who know that it is Jesus' empowering presence working on the inside of them that gives them great value. They have done some spiritual mathematics. By adding up what Jesus means to them and, by refusing to trust their possessions, they subtract that which prevents them knowing him fully. In this way they have discovered the pearl of great price. If we believe our identity is like a buried treasure (Matthew 13:44) then we too will trade everything in order to find ourselves.

To enter into the important agenda that God has for us we will have to make life changing decisions. Escaping the frantic pace of pursuing the urgent will cost us something. We each pay a price for side-stepping the distractions of the world and entering the place where Jesus waits. The price we pay is a refusal to be conformed into the world's pattern. Are you refusing to be pushed about by pulsating demands that have nothing to do with God's will for you?

## *Waiting on God*

Spending time with Jesus ignites a passion in our heart. *"Didn't our hearts burn within us?"* asked the two men walking with Jesus on the Emmaus road (Luke 24:32). Opening our hearts up to God allows the brilliance of his inner qualities to touch the deepest parts of our being. As we allow God's light to shine on us he will show us what we are truly like.

We will never enter into all that God has for us by looking into the deceptive mirrors of the world. If we want to discover our own identity apart from God we will lose everything. But if we give up our own ideas of what love and happiness look like and follow Jesus then we will discover our true identity.

## Consider

- When we first come into the secret place we will need to slow down. Why?
- Escaping the frantic pace of pursuing the urgent will cost us something. Why, and what will it cost you?
- What prevents you from connecting with God?

*God rewrote the text of my life*
*When I opened the book*
*of my heart to his eyes.* [85]

# Thirty Two

# Is There Anyone Out There?

*Call to me and I will answer you and tell you great and*
*unsearchable things you do not know.*
(Jeremiah 33:3 NIV)

## *Hearing God's voice prevents discouragement*

*T*o live successful lives it is vital that we hear God speaking. God has placed within each of us the capacity to hear his voice. He desires that we pay attention to what he is saying. Some of us may be asking, "Why is it so important that we hear God speaking anyway?" It is important because our identity is connected to hearing his voice. Jesus said, "My sheep hear my voice and they follow me" (John 10:4).

But many live far from this ideal, and some even believe it is normal not to hear God's voice. How hard would it be to develop a friendship with someone you could never speak to or with whom you could not hear? Sometimes lovers just sit in silence, but it would hardly be a relationship if they never spoke to each other. Most of us read the Bible without ever going into the secret place and seeking him face to face. God does not want us to follow him from a distance. Rather he desires that we hear the rhythm of his extraordinary thoughts beating within his heart.

## *Does God want to speak to me?*

Do we feel significant when his voice imparts acceptance and love? Of course we do. God made us to be in relationship with him so we could especially hear him speaking to us. God has a mind, will and emotions and behind his voice is one who thinks and feels. His voice is an expression of himself. When I hear God's voice, I understand more of who I really am. His voice enables us to believe that we are precious.

Is God speaking to you? Are you listening? When we hear God's voice our response to difficult situation is altered and we become bigger on the inside. *"Listen for God's voice in everything you do, everywhere you go; he's the one who will keep you on track."*[86] We are on a journey to discover our true identity. God's voice prevents us getting lost. Do you remember the last time when you felt refreshed by God's gentle words? The gentle spoken whisper from God's heart makes us feel significant even when we are not doing anything to impress.

## God hears our spoken prayers

Often we speak to God not even being sure that he hears us. In the past there have been many times that I have spoken to God whilst being unaware of his listening ear. How many times have you prayed and yet felt that God was ignoring you with selective deafness?

God does not ignore us. God hears both our spoken and unspoken prayers with the eyes of his heart. I remember praying a prayer inviting God to be exalted over my comforts, friends, ambitions, reputation, likes and dislikes, my family, my health, and even my life itself.[87] I really had no idea that God was listening and he would take my prayer seriously. Within a couple of months of praying that prayer, I arrived in the Solomon Islands where I had no comforts and no friends. My reputation of being a balanced Christian was challenged,

> *The key to reflecting Jesus' image is a deep intimate relationship with him.*

my likes and dislikes ignored and my ambition became one of survival. In hearing my prayer with the eyes of his heart he took me to a place where he could answer that prayer.

## God hears our unspoken prayers

God has an intense desire to hear his children. He *looks* into our hearts and *hears* our unspoken prayers. I remember being stranded in Honiara for two weeks with no belongings and little money. We had come over to see my parents off after their visit to us in the Solomon Islands and we were ready to travel back to Onepusu by boat that night. We were told the boat would leave at six fifteen that night. Arriving at the wharf an hour before the departure time, we were startled to see the boat chugging out from the wharf. We had loaded our gear into the boat that afternoon and we only had a smidgen of hand luggage with us. I was so stunned that I could not verbalise my thoughts. However, God heard my unspoken prayer for insight and that night he spoke to me from a devotional book and said:

> I am thy shield. Have no fear; you must know that all is well. I will never let anyone do to you both other than My will for you. I can see the future. I can read man's hearts. I know better than you do what you need. Trust me absolutely. You are not at the mercy of fate, or buffeted about by others. You are being led in a very definite way and I am moving others who do not serve your purpose out of your path. Never fear, what ever may happen. You are both being led. Do not try to plan. I have planned …. Trust Me, your very extremity will ensure My activity for you. [88]

The next day Brian tried to make plans. Oh how he tried. Every one of those plans fell through as God moved out of our path those that did not serve our purpose. In hindsight, we had the best holiday of our entire six years during those two weeks when all we could do was rest.

## *The power of looking*

No-one has ever seen God and lived. Many misunderstand what actually dies when we see God. The old self in us cannot live in the presence of God. It withers and dies when standing within the realm of his goodness. When we see God we begin to live for someone bigger than ourselves. Although God is a Spirit, the Bible clearly tells us that we can see his face. Psalm 123:2 says that we should look to the Lord our God till he shows us his mercy. Looking carries with it the idea of waiting. If I were at a bus stop waiting for a bus, I would keep my eyes on the look out for its arrival. If I closed my eyes, it is likely that I would

> *Developing the art of 'looking' is an important part of listening*

miss the bus. So it is with God. If we are to hear him, we need to keep our eyes open so that we can see him. We may ask, "What does it mean to look to God with our eyes?" Tom, with a penetrating gaze, would look straight into people's eyes and say, "Look at me," when he wanted to say something important. Somehow, I hear God saying these same words to all of us. Hearing God involves turning the inner eyes of our heart towards him. The word *look* means, "to turn one's eyes in some direction, to contemplate, to examine and to make a visual or mental search."[89]

When we look to God in this way we can hear him speak to us. Looking to God lets him know that we are paying attention. Further to this, looking is synonymous with believing.[90]

## *Seeking his face in silence*

*One thing I ask of the Lord,*
*This is what I seek:*
*That I may dwell in the house of the Lord*
*All the days of my life*
*To gaze upon the beauty of the Lord*
*And to seek him in his temple.*

*For in the day of trouble*
*He will keep me safe in his dwelling;*
*He will hide me in the shelter of his tabernacle*
*And set me high upon a rock.* (Psalm 27: 4-5 NV)

All distractions are silenced when we gaze on the face of God. We can come to God and do all the talking and think we have achieved a relationship. God has trained me in the power of looking in silence. I have learnt to quieten my thoughts and look into his face with my inner eyes. At the time that he taught me to do this I was a busy mum with three small children. We do not have to be physically still to gaze into the heart of God. We do, however, have to discover that there are inner eyes in our heart that can be directed towards heaven to see him at anytime of the day or night. To my astonishment as I lifted my inner eyes towards him I discovered that he was looking back at me! It started at first with just a glance, but I felt noticed. Those little glances throughout the day became more frequent until they developed into a look with intent. I found myself gazing on the heart of God. I did all this in silence. As I looked into his heart I was surprised to hear him speaking.

> *His voice is life changing, inspiring and invigorating. It refreshes and imparts life.*

Developing the art of 'looking' is an important part of listening. We are unique and special. Have you ever become aware of the eyes of God looking into your soul? I love it when I become aware that God is looking at me. I recognise his look and I know I have his attention, but more than that, his gaze acknowledges that I am important to him. He is a living image (*eikon*) reflector.[91] When God and I exchange a glance something of his nature penetrates my soul. That changes me. I found that when God shone his light into my heart, he was giving me something of himself. I felt his love, tenderness and compassion.

When his likeness touches the core of our being false messages, icons and negative imagery eventually fades. God's vision removes the fog of self-doubt lingering around our lives and makes everything clear. Seeing yourself through the mirror of God's eyes will convince you of your worth, significance and value.

If we take the time to gaze upon God we will see an exact likeness of our true identity. I have a friend who had a vision of Jesus. As she gazed on his magnificence, she felt she had nothing to give him in comparison to his splendour. He then asked her to give him her emptiness. She did that and since that time I have seen an amazing strength and endurance within her. By giving us individual attention Jesus has the power to change us.

As we make a visual search to hear we will be surprised to see how insightful and magnificently he speaks. The language of heaven is the language of knowing in our heart. God's voice is heard with the inner antenna of our hearts. His voice is life changing, inspiring and invigorating. It refreshes and imparts life. His voice re-energizes and rekindles passion. His voice reminds us of our beauty and reconnects us to the power source of the Holy Spirit. His voice is incredibly tender and provokes a feeling of being loved. As we turn our eyes towards God and consider what he is saying, our faith and confidence increase. The concept of looking to hear is found in the book of James. James says that as we look into the perfect law we hear what we see.

> But the man who **looks** intently into the perfect law that gives freedom, and continues to do this, not forgetting what he has heard, but doing it - *he will be blessed in what he does.* (James 1: 25 NIV)

Throughout Scripture, we are encouraged to look to God. Psalm 4:6 says, *"Let the light of your face shine upon us, O Lord."* We are encouraged to *"Look to the Lord and his strength; seek his face always"* (Psalm 105:4 NIV). When we look to God we will understand that he always desires to speak. As we seek his face we see his smile and hear his words of approval. The face of God communicates peace and acceptance.

## Consider

- How does God hear us with his eyes?
- What does it mean to look to God?
- Have you ever become aware of the eyes of God looking into your soul?
- Explain what happens when God touches the core of our being with his Spirit.

# Thirty Three

# Rejecting Distorted Voices

273

"Hi Linda,"

"No, it's Kerrie."

"Oh you sound just like your sister. Can I speak with Linda?"

"Sure, I'll get her!"

*H*ow many times do we mistake one person for another? It's a bit like speaking with God. We often confuse his voice with that of ourselves, or the voice of fear or circumstance. However, I never mistake Brian's voice on the phone. We have been married thirty years so I have intimate knowledge of his voice. Similarly, the more we speak with God and listen to him the more we will be able to discern his voice.

Adam and Eve were friends with God and spoke with him often, yet they were seduced by a voice that propelled mankind into a realm of darkness. Today, the problem is not that we cannot hear it is just that we have become captivated by other voices. We cannot hear the right voice.

## *How can I hear God?*

The voices that speak to us from within the mirrors of the world system can be silenced by the gentle whisper of God. God has taught me to look to him in five ways so that I can hear his voice speaking. These ways include:

- praising God
- worship
- blessing our enemies
- developing a relationship with the Holy Spirit
- speaking the Word over our situations.

Let's explore each of these ways in some detail.

# Praising God

*He who sacrifices thank offerings honours me*
*and he prepares the way so that I may show him*
*the salvation of God.* (Psalm 50:23 NIV)

There are many voices that deafen our ears to God's voice. The voices of negativity and trouble have power to silence the voice of God. Often our circumstances speak louder to us than the still small voice of God.

Praising God silences the negativity that prevents us experiencing a breakthrough in our situations. When the voice of punishment boomed within the walls of the prison cell, Paul and Silas silenced its voice with praise. Instead of feeling sorry for themselves by focusing on their situation they sang praises and focused on the all-powerful king of the universe. In response God sent an earthquake that opened the prison doors. In that moment they heard with the eyes of their understanding that God was all-powerful. Our praises can open the doors that are preventing us moving forward. We find God's perfect will when we thank him (1 Thessalonians 5:18). Gratitude is the language of heaven and releases supernatural power. Thanking God releases the angels in the heavenly realm to fight for us in the earthly realm.

> *God feels welcome when we give him a standing ovation in times of difficulties.*

God feels welcome when we give him a standing ovation in times of difficulties. Praising Jesus directs our focus away from the problem and onto him. Many times I have faced situations that required divine interventions. Our youngest daughter became critically ill when she was only six weeks old. That night I lay in my bed determined to praise God according to Habakkuk 3:16. I praised God day and night in those early days and the doctor referred to her as a miracle baby for surviving such an ordeal. Today Libby is a healthy, vibrant, young woman. Praising Jesus enables us to hear his voice and see his power in our lives.

## *Worship*

Worship silences the voice of idols that demand our adoration. We worship and place high value on the things that promise significance. Worship is what some guys do with their cars and most girls do with their bodies. We worship the very thing that gives us value! We venerate, respect, adore and are passionate about the things that reflect our image.

> *As I lifted my inner eyes towards God, I discovered that he was looking back at me!*

Because we allow our cars and bodies to speak to us concerning our worth we often forget that in doing so we worship the creature rather than the unseen Creator.

We are designed to worship the One who would reflect back to us our image. We are designed to worship God, not only because he is worthy of our worship, but also because he alone can give us a deep clear view of ourselves. Is it possible to think about Jesus more than anything else? Is that being too spiritual and heavenly minded so that we are of no earthly use? My conviction is that it is not! When we behold God by focusing on him, his very likeness is reflected back onto our spirit.

Placing high value on God creates an atmosphere around our lives that enables us to hear him speaking. Throughout the Old Testament, we see worship preceding a breakthrough of silence from God. When we declare who God is in worship we begin to hear him speaking. Worship is giving God the worth he is due and creates an atmosphere around us that he loves to invade.

## *Open hearts*

So how do we go from worshipping our cars and bodies to worshipping Jesus? We cross this bridge by opening our hearts up to God. The worship in the church I attend is phenomenal and yet I am aware that there are those who keep their hearts closed. Have you ever been at church and kept your heart closed in worship? "Well God I'm singing here to you, but I just want to enjoy a few moments to myself." Or "I don't like the songs we are singing; they're too boring ... too fast ... too loud ... too soft." Or we could get thinking about what that person said to us last week and what we are going to have for lunch. One friend told me that she would be going through the motions but in her heart, she was bored and distracted. She would look around to see with whom she must catch up!

We were made to enjoy God's company and opening our hearts to him in worship brings us into his very presence. When we look into his heart through adoration we will encounter his voice speaking to us. But the problem is that many of us have built high and impenetrable walls between ourselves and God, preventing us seeing him face to face. Not understanding that he stands on the other side waiting for us to remove the unbelief in our hearts, we feel that he is more distant than what he really is. God can only be invited into our world as much as we are prepared to tear down the walls preventing him access.

## *Music*

Even in the midst of impossible language barriers, a smile

communicates love and acceptance. Like a smile, music is a universal language. Wherever we go, whatever culture we are in, music will always remain the language of the heart. It has power to speak straight to our soul, stirring our emotions. Because we can easily access music, worship is a lifestyle to be lived and therefore is not restricted to church. I often listen to a worship Cd and smell the fragrance of his presence. God speaks to me through the songs and reinforces his love and care over my life. Lyrics have the power to speak to our hearts, not just our minds. An invisible spiritual force is connected from our hearts to what and whom we worship. God longs to be with us. Lingering in his presence gives us a greater chance to hear him; it opens our ears to his voice. Have you ever had coffee with God - where you sat down and opened up your heart to him? Passion for Jesus and worshipping him has nothing to do with our personalities. It is simply unbolting the door to our hearts and allowing him to come in.

## Blessing our enemies

Negative imagery can muffle the voice of God. Often it is in the practical everyday life that God prepares our hearts to hear him. We desire life to be hassle free but this may mean missing the very opportunities that God gives us to reflect his image and so develop a capacity to hear him. Being aware of our responses in the battle of daily life and overcoming such obstacles prevents negative imagery being developed in our minds.

A couple of years ago I began leading a group of intercessors and teaching them how to stand in the battle. Each week I worked very hard on my own heart to overcome obstacles by blessing my enemies. Then as we met I was amazed at the level of God's presence in the group and how easy it was for me to hear clearly from the Holy Spirit. The Bible says, *"Blessed are the pure in heart for they shall see God"* (Matthew 5: 8 NIV). Pure hearts are shaped in an atmosphere of intimacy with Jesus. Blessing our enemies silences the voices of hate and resentment that prevent us hearing God. When we bless our enemies we can recognise his voice and hear what he is saying.

## Relationship with the Holy Spirit

In the Old Testament God had promised that he would be with his people. *"This is what I covenanted with you when you came out from Egypt. And My spirit remains among you"* (Haggai 2:5 NIV). Like a faithful father comforting his child, God's presence became a source of hope to his people. Even in the Old Testament, long before the Holy Spirit was released into the hearts of men and women in the New, people recognised that the *"spirit of the holy gods"* was with Daniel (Daniel 4:8). It was by his Spirit that the people would defeat their enemy (Zechariah 4:6 NIV). Even though God had promised his presence to be continually with his people, it is clear that the Holy Spirit lived in heaven (John 7:39). Yet the day would come when God would pour out his Spirit on all flesh (Joel 2:28). The Holy Spirit would become our eyes enabling us to see and understand the things of the Spirit.

> *God can only be invited into our world as much as we are prepared to tear down the walls preventing him access.*

When Jesus died and returned to heaven God released the Holy Spirit into the world. God has placed his own Spirit within us and invites us into a personal relationship so that we can understand how we are made. *"In him, we live and have our being"* (Acts 17:28), speaks of an interchange of thought, will and desire. It is within the realm of this amazing interchange that we can understand our true identity. The key to reflecting God's image is a deep intimate relationship with Jesus through the power of the Holy Spirit.

We encounter God through relationship with the Holy Spirit who transforms us by revealing God's heart to us. To hear God clearly it is vital we come into relationship with the Holy Spirit. The Holy Spirit is the third member of the Godhead and has now been released into the world. He is known as the Helper, the Advocate, the Counsellor and the Comforter. The Holy Spirit lives in the hearts of believers and brings power and boldness into their lives. He is described as a rushing wind (John 3:8). Like the wind we cannot see the Holy Spirit but we can feel him and see the results of his presence. He whispers God's love into our spirit by gently transcribing God's words into our hearts. He turns the light on so we can see clearly.

We can learn to tune our hearts into the frequency of his voice. Stunning life changing encounters are experienced through the profound tenderness of the Holy Spirit (Psalm 18:35).

*The Spirit searches all things, even the deep things of God. For who among men knows the thoughts of a man except the man's spirit within him? In the same way no-one knows the thoughts of God except the Spirit of God. We have not received the sprit of the world but the spirit who is from God, that we might understand what God has freely given us.* (1 Corinthians 2:7-12 NIV)

## Speaking God's Word

*The voice of the Lord ...*
*breaks in pieces the cedars of Lebanon ...*
*The voice of the Lord strikes with flashes of lightning.*
*The voice of the Lord shakes the desert.*

*The voice of the Lord twists the oaks, strips the forest bare
and in his temple all cry "Glory!"*
(Psalm 29: 3-5 and 7-8 NIV)

Speaking God's word over our situation intimidates the enemy; it silences his voice. The Word of God opens our eyes to the magnitude of God's estimation of us and is a mirror that reflects back to us a perfect picture of our true identity. We need to capture that picture and allow it to shape us into becoming who God says we are. We capture the image God has of us when we believe it.

The Word of God penetrates the deepest part of our being; it separates what we think in our heads with what we believe in our hearts (Hebrews 4:12). Many of us believe one thing in our head, usually based on the Word, and at the same time we believe an altogether different thing in our emotions (based on what people say). The Bible delineates this for us. For example, perhaps we don't believe God will provide for us, but we read in his Word that he *"will meet all your needs according to his glorious riches in Christ Jesus"* (Philippians 4:19 NIV). Believing God's Word, even in the midst of our struggles, gives room for God to powerfully work miracles in our lives. Whatever our situation God has already provided the answer.

I remember praying for a friend who had been sick for many years. We had been doing some warfare over his ministry and at the end of that time God simply spoke to me and gave me a strategy for healing. Through the word spoken that night a miracle was released into his life and he was healed. Often we underestimate both the creative and destructive powers within the voice of God. Jesus calls things that are not yet in existence into being with his voice and yet at the same time is able to destroy the powers of darkness. The Word of God enables us to engage in warfare; it is a powerful sword.

Using his voice, God created the universe out of nothing.

He created order out of chaos. We can recreate order out of our chaos when we declare his Word over our situations. God's voice is powerful and mighty as it thunders over the impossible situations in our lives. It strikes as lightning to obliterate and smash every obstacle. It twists and breaks the unyielding and stubborn blockages to our growth and it calms the troubled waters in our life.

## God's deliverance

When we speak the Word of God over our problems we will see God act. Intimacy and hearing his voice will give us confidence to resist the principalities and powers in the heavenly realm that are against us. God's Word becomes alive and is able to change our world when we speak it out over our circumstances. With the sword of the Spirit, which is the quickened Word of God in our mouth, we can see strongholds demolished at the sound of his voice.

There is nothing more alarming to the enemy than the voice of the Lord spoken through you as you declare Scripture to the spirit realm. Next time fear grips we can declare this scripture over our situation, *"God has not given you a spirit of fear but of power and of love and a sound mind"* (2 Timothy 1: 7 KJV), and then watch your enemy flee at the sound of God's Word spoken through you.

As we speak God's Word out in faith, we will see him demonstrating his all-powerful hand over our problems. The enemy shudders when he sees a child of God coming with the quickened Word in his mouth. God declares that his Word is now in our mouth, we need to wield that sword of his Word on our own behalf and on behalf of those whom we love (Deuteronomy 30:14).

A couple of years ago, after a period of intense warfare, God said to me, "From now on everything you do will be from a sitting position." Over time I began to understand that even the hardest of challenges that I faced in the spirit realm I was able to overcome just by coming into agreement with God. It was as if I was sitting down resting and he was doing all the hard work. God's power is activated each time we agree with him. God, who rules and reigns from heaven, has placed his Spirit within us so that we can make the right choice in every situation. It is possible to become the shining lights we are intended to be in this dark world.

Hearing God's voice develops friendship with him and enables us to receive an insightful understanding of our worth. God is waiting in the secret place to speak with you. In speaking with you he will mirror his thoughts into your heart and a greater understanding of his awesomeness will be imprinted into your spirit.

## *Consider*

- What are the five ways that we can look to God so that we are able to hear him speak?
- Explain how the Holy Spirit can impact our lives?

*Don't be intimidated. Eventually everything is going to be out in the open, and everyone will know how things really are. So don't hesitate to go public now. Don't be bluffed into silence by the threats of bullies."*[94]

# Thirty Four

# Intimacy Transforms Us into Warriors

*Praise the Lord who is my rock.*
*He trains my hands for war and my fingers for battle.*
*He is my loving ally and my fortress, my tower of safety, my*
*rescuer. He is my shield and I take refuge in him. He makes*
*nations submit to me.*
(Psalm 144:1-2 NLT)

*Great peace have those who love your law*
*and nothing causes them to stumble.*
(Psalm 119:165 NKJV)

## *Worship destroys intimidation*

*G*od is raising up an army of worshippers. He is creating for himself a people who will praise him. Jesus has won the war and our identity can be now found in him. God's ways are perfect and all his promises are true. He is a shield to all those who look to him for protection (Psalm 18). We will grow up into the full stature of Christ when we build images of God's powerful greatness into our identity.

We are winners, the enemy is defeated. We can live with our heads held high. No weapon formed against us will prosper and we will shine like lights in this world and in the world to come.

David experienced these truths and received his identity from God alone. He became king and fought many battles that ultimately displayed God's power on his behalf.

> *For who is God except the Lord? Who but our God is a solid rock ... He **trains** my hand for battle; he **strengthens** my arm to draw a bronze bow. You have given me your shield of victory. Your right hand **supports** me; your help has made me great. You have made a wide path for my feet to keep them from slipping.* (Psalm 18:30-36 NLT)

The NIV Bible translates "*your help has made me great*" with "*your gentleness has made me great*". God shares the truth with us in such a gentle way that we are able to understand how it relates to us. He speaks gently drawing us to himself. He explains that by dismantling lies we disarm the enemy and remove his weaponry. Such gentleness empowers us to become great before our enemies.

God trains our hands for battle by firstly raising us up as worshippers and then by training us to utilise truth as a weapon. Incorporating truth into our identity gives us the upper hand which enables us to walk confidently. *"God's spirit touches our spirit and confirms who we really are"*[95]

"Nothing great has ever been achieved except by those who dared to believe something inside them was superior to circumstances."[96] The seed of greatness has been planted deep within each of us. But the question remains: what is greatness? Is it becoming a famous astronaut or a renowned journalist? Is it becoming a legendary pioneer trekking the jungles of South America? Greatness, according to God, is found in having an overcoming spirit that refuses defeat.

> *Allow God to captivate your heart, and to gently teach you to use the truth as a weapon.*

There are many unsung heroes who have learnt the secret to becoming great in the midst of tremendous disappointments. These people are not overwhelmed by difficulties. They have the inner resources to tackle their problems. I have deep admiration for people who face life head on. They might consider themselves to be failures, but they are winners. Having a focused purpose and refusing to give up makes these people heroes.

Suguhara, a Japanese diplomat in the Second World War, faced a crossroad when his government refused to give him permission to grant visas to the Jews fleeing the horrors of Lithuania. At that crossroad, he rose up to become a great man by refusing to give up. Finally, knowing that his decision would cost him his job; he defied his government and issued thousands of visas. Subsequently many escaped impending death and thousands of precious lives were saved. The Jews arrived safely in Japan and then were later shipped to China when Japan became allies with Germany. Suguhara dared to believe that something inside of him was greater than his circumstances. A desire to honour God above man gave him victory in the battle of words and made him a hero.

David knew God to be great. He had experienced the wonder of the cosmos as he lay under the stars in the wilds. He had seen God's greatness deliver him from the jaws of lions and bears.

> *Greatness, according to God, is found in having an overcoming spirit that refuses defeat.*

It was in this place of obscurity that he learnt to become a worshipping warrior who persevered. The more captivated he became with God's greatness, the more determined he was to defy his enemies. With his focus fixed on God he refused to be overwhelmed. David became great because he mirrored a great God.

"*But the people who know their God shall be strong and carry out great exploits*" (Daniel 11:32 NKJV). The word *exploit* carries with it ideas of "brilliant achievements and utilizing and taking advantage of the situation."[99]

David took advantage of the situation when he entered onto the battlefield with some lunch for his brothers. On arriving he was surprised to see the army in disarray, running from a giant. Even in the face of a lion David never ran. David, in seeing the situation for what it was, decided to get involved. Feeling the stirrings of conquest on the inside of him he offered to slay the giant. Saul, of course, was happy that someone had stepped up displaying such bravery. To aid his effort, he insisted that he use his armour.

David's older brother Eliab on the other hand, demanded that he return home. There are times we may have decided to push through all the barriers. At our point of breakthrough, we may find ourselves being challenged by those who fail to see destiny in our lives. When the hecklers are hot on our heels, just like David, we need to push through the obstacles. The resolve within David allowed him to ignore all the jeering and, throwing away Saul's armour, he picked up five smooth stones from a stream and placed them in his shepherd's bag.

Because David had intimate knowledge of the One who was greater than any foe, he was confident (1 Samuel 17 -18). When everyone else was looking *up* at Goliath as he shouted life defying threats, David was looking *down* at him. Refusing to entertain destructive threats he ignored the bullying and, armed with faith in God, confidently faced his opponent.

> "*Goliath walked out towards David with his shield bearer ahead of him, sneering in contempt at this ruddy boy. 'Am I a dog,' he roared at David, 'that you come to me with a stick?' and he cursed David by the name of his gods. 'Come over here, and I'll give your flesh to the birds and wild animals!' Goliath yelled.*
>
> *'You come to me with a sword, spear and javelin, but I come to you in the name of the Lord Almighty – the God of the armies of Israel, who you have defied. Today the Lord will conquer you, and I will kill you and cut off your head. And then I will give the bodies of your men to the birds and wild animals and the whole world will know that there is a God in Israel! And everyone will know that the Lord does not need weapons to rescue his people, it is His battle, not ours. The Lord will give you to us.' As Goliath moved closer to attack, David quickly ran out to meet him, reaching into his shepherd's bag and taking out a stone, he hurled it from his sling and hit the Philistine in the forehead. The stone sank in and Goliath stumbled and fell face down to the ground.*"
> (1 Samuel 17:42-49 NLT)

David, captivated by God, took advantage of every situation that he faced to reveal that he was a reflector of God's power. I *chased my enemies and caught them. I did not stop until they were conquered. I struck them down so they could not get up. They fell beneath my feet* (Psalm 18:37-38 NLT). Are you revealing God's power as you face your goliaths in the arena of offence, sickness or strained friendships? Or have you compared yourself to the size of your challenge, and instead of destroying the imagery, run away?

There will be many giants to face as God reshapes our character into his likeness. Giants will cause us to doubt our worth by making us appear small. Giants will convince us that God isn't as big as he says he is. There will be giants of the past that demand that we conform to their view of us. We should not dwarfed by this imagery. We are told that we sit with Jesus far above principalities and powers (Ephesians 1:5). We are seated in the heavenly realm. From that standpoint, the giants in our world should look like grasshoppers.

King David was raised out of a place of obscurity to a place where he was great before his enemies. When we rise up and challenge our goliaths, we too can see our enemy fall beneath our feet.

When the enemy challenges our identity we can take advantage of the situtation by coming against him in a power that is far greater than our own. Understanding that nothing can destroy our worth enables us to push through all our barriers and rise up in an adventurous spirit. The bigger we are on the inside, the easier it will be to defeat intimidation. We can't make intimidation fall if we are small in our own eyes. If we are small in our own eyes we will measure ourselves against the situation intimidating us. Do you know what I mean? The *bigger* the situation, the *smaller* on the inside we become. We destroy our giants by comparing their size with the size of God and by destroying the fear of the unknown with the promise that God will never leave us nor forsake us.

We might think that it is well and good for David to rise up and kill Goliath because we remember him as a mighty warrior, a famous psalmist and a valiant king. Before David killed Goliath, he had his own personal self-esteem battles to face. He was not recognised as a legitimate member of his family. When Samuel came to anoint one of the sons of Jesse with oil for kingship David was overlooked in the line up so someone had to go out and find him. After he rose to be king, he then went on to face many situations that would have spoken negative messages about his worth. On numerous occasions David had entire armies come against him in battle. He fell into adultery. His own son committed treason against him. David had plenty of reasons to doubt his worth and to see himself as insignificant. The Psalms are his personal record of such inner turmoil.

It was only as David confronted his own self-doubt that he was able to rise up and overcome his difficulties. Through seeking God's opinion during times of intimidation, David discovered that *"fear of God builds up confidence."*[97] We develop a healthy fear of God when we respect his opinion above the opinion of man. *Fear of God is a spring of living water, so you won't go off drinking from poisonous wells."*[98] David faced threats many times, yet by seeking God he built himself up in the Lord (1 Samuel 30:6). He discovered an inner strength as he gained a greater understanding of who he was in God's eyes. As he learnt to build strong internal structures of inner worth and value he rose to become a man full of faith and power.

> *Even in the worst situations, if we connect to the God of the "I can", we will become all that God planned for us to be.*

Ross learnt to become great before his enemy when he was transferred out of a very comfortable teaching position in the country to the city. Every time I saw him and his wife at church in my mind I saw Ross dressed in armour holding a sword in one hand and a shield in the other. When I asked God about the vision, he told me that he was training Ross's "hands for war and his fingers for battle."

Months after the transfer I discovered that Ross was having difficulties and this depressed him. I encouraged him saying, "God is raising you as a warrior. Fight and don't get depressed." God saw a warrior spirit imprinted within Ross's eternal blueprint, yet Ross only saw his own weakness. Even though the situation made Ross doubt his worth, he rose up and became the warrior that God had made him to be. As Ross took up the weapons of war he discovered that God was there ready to fight on his behalf. God specifically used that particular adventure to train him into becoming the person he designed him in ages past to be.

> *Faith in God's opinion allows us to see clearly all the wonderful characteristics he has placed within us.*

God made us to make known that he is the God of the impossible. To reflect him perfectly however, we need to gain a vision of his greatness. Even in the worst situations, if we connect ourselves to the God of the "I can" we will become all that God planned us to be. We are winners not losers.

Using your spiritual DNA, take advantage of your situation and reveal God's power. Allow God to captivate your heart, allow him to teach you how to use the truth as a weapon. Allow God to influence the way you see yourself. Be like David and take advantage of the size of your problem. The bigger your problem the easier it will be not to miss your target when you come against it! This will make you great.

## Who are your goliaths?

Are you like David? Do you know that you have power to destroy sickness, depression, poverty, fear and resentment that plague our worlds? *"The lives of good people are brightly lit streets."*[100] We are reflectors of light. We need the tenacity to stand up and refuse the dark imagery the world throws at us. Even though we have grown up allowing others to define us, it is now our responsibility to embrace the image that God has of us. We do this by adjusting our vision so that we see ourselves from God's perspective. Receiving revelation from God enables us to see the obstacles preventing us overcoming our difficulties. *You, O lord, keep my lamp burning; my God turns my darkness into light. With your help I can advance against a troop; with my God I can scale a wall* (Psalm 18:28-29 NIV). Faith in God's opinion allows us to see clearly all the wonderful characteristics he has placed within us.

## Consider

- Do you allow lies to affect your self-image?
- Do you use your God given power to destroy all the giants of negativity that mar your image?
- Are you removing negativity from your heart so that you are able to overcome intimidation?

A little bit of fragrance, Lord,
That's what I want to be,
I want to spread your perfume round,
And share your Life in Me
What a truly lovely perfume
You would channel through to all,
If the fullness of your spirit
Like a shower, began to fall.

Fill me as an empty vessel,
Pour your fragrant life in me,
Send me forth with your aroma,
And your spirit wafting free.

Joan Gooda

# Thirty Five

# Reflectors

Would you like
an
encounter with Jesus
that will change
your
world?

## Are you captivated by God?

*T*here is nothing more gratifying nor more piercing than the gaze of God. His gaze imparts to us power to prosper and succeed. It gives direction and answers our questions. Many throughout the Bible have discovered their true identity while *encountering* Jesus face to face.

## Encounters in the wilderness

The Samaritan woman, looking to find her identity in relationships with men, had no idea that she would find the mirror of her true image when she escaped the crowd and, in the heat of the day, drew water from the well outside the city gates. This woman was a throw-away to society. Her lifestyle had sidelined her, and deep down she felt that she didn't matter. Little did she realise that her world would change through a simple conversation with Jesus. Initially, in finding out that Jesus knew about her life, terrified her. But as the conversation gained momentum; the rush of adrenalin and sheer lack of control became exhilarating. Then, as if savouring the view of the mountaintop summit, the woman discovered something she had been desperately looking for and had thought she would never find - the unattainable sense of worth and dignity. She was so impressed with the journey that she invited others to join her; a whole village responded and broke out in revival (John 4:39-41).

People got it wrong about the woman and they can get it wrong about us. They can stick labels on us that are poles apart from who God says we are. They can say that we will never reach our potential and that our past will always stain our image. Has anyone said such a thing to you and now those words have stuck in your mind preventing you from becoming the person God made you to be? Have such words caused you to make adjustments to how you see yourself; blurring your real identity of being loved and righteous?

People got it wrong about John when he was dumped on the island of Patmos. He had been sent there "because of the Word of God and the testimony of Jesus" (Revelation 1: 9 NIV). In other words, he was there as a punishment for being a brilliant light. This didn't faze him and was worshipping on the Lord's Day when he heard a voice speaking to him.

*"I turned around to see the voice that was speaking to me. And when I turned, I saw seven golden lamp stands, and among them someone like the Son of Man, dressed in a robe reaching down to His feet, and with a golden sash around His chest. His head and hair were like wool as white as snow and His eyes were like blazing fire. His feet were like bronze glowing in a furnace and His voice like the sound of rushing waters. In His right hand, He held seven stars and out of His mouth came a sharp double-edged sword. His face was like the sun shining in all its brilliance."* (Revelations 1:12-16 NIV)

> *Even though we have grown up allowing others to define us, it is now our responsibility to embrace the image that God has of us.*

John, when he turned to see the voice speaking to him, was completely ruined for ordinary living (Revelations 1:17). Do you want to be ruined like that? Would you like an encounter with Jesus that will change your world?

Moses, whilst wandering in the desert, was drawn aside by a burning bush. The flames roared but the bush wasn't consumed. As Moses came near to take a closer look, he heard a voice saying. *"Do not come any closer,"* God said, *"Take off your sandals for the ground where you are standing is holy ground"* (Exodus 3:5

NIV). Up until that point Moses had been protecting a wounded self-image. He had killed an Egyptian and was running from his crime. But then a burning bush refocused Moses attention. Through speaking to Moses within its flame, God captivated Moses affections and renewed his purpose. From that point on, Moses refused to go anywhere without God's presence. When called to take the children out of Egypt, Moses reminded God that he needed his presence. *"If your presence does not go with us, do not send us up from here"* (Exodus 33:15 NIV).

> *Passion for God is a doorway that leads us into a deeper understanding of our true identity.*

Moses, after having spent forty days on the mountain, was so captivated by God that his face shone so brightly that he had to cover it (Exodus 34:35). After hearing God's voice, Moses was ready to respond. No longer relying on his willpower and strength; he relied on someone greater. The heavenly voice awakened his affections and opened his mind to the possibility of living for Someone superior to himself. Through continual encounters with God Moses rose to become the person God always intended him to be.

## Paul

Paul became a reflector of God when he was struck to the ground by an intense light from heaven (Acts 9:1-5). At the time he was travelling to Damascus to find, and then kill, the Christians. He was a religious fanatic who lost sight of mercy and compassion. Jesus broke into his self-focused world with a question that changed his life. A voice within a blinding light changed his life. He became captivated by someone more powerful and loving than himself.

More recently, Ian McCormack had an unexpected encounter with God in the midst of a hectic social life. He was stung by a box jelly fish and consequently died and went to heaven. He recalls the life-changing experience:

"White light pierced through the darkness and I was enclosed in intense light. Waves of light, comfort, peace and joy all were encapsulated in a radiant beam of light I realised that here there were no shadows, God sees everything. Pure, underserved love washed over me, wave after wave began to pour over me. God's love intensified as I told God about my sins. The dignity of my face was lifted up - I was encased in white light – he forgave all my sins. Awe and respect for him was drawn out of me by his love. His healing presence penetrated the core of my being."[92]

## *Captivated*

Just as living in luxury spoils us, so being captivated by Jesus makes the things of the world desperately inadequate to describe our worth. One glimpse of God's image and the sound of his voice changed every distorted self-perception within these men. Their lives were totally transformed by a speaking voice that didn't come from a mythical world, but rather came from their place of origin.

The key to discovering our worth is to become captivated by God. *"If your first concern is to look after yourself, you'll never find yourself. But if you forget about yourself and look to me, you'll find both yourself and me."*[93] We become passionate by whatever captivates us. What do you think about? What pleases you? Whatever gives us pleasure, significance, or meets our deep need to be loved, will captivate our affections. If the devil can steal our affections by getting us to focus on ourselves, he will capture our desire and ensnare our will. He will entice us to walk away from God.

Passion for God is a doorway that leads us into a deeper

understanding of our true identity. When we set our affections on things above, we will then repent of looking for our identity in the things of the world. Paul tells us to, *"Set your mind on things above and not on earthly things"* (Colossians 3:2NIV). Life-changing power and pleasure are found in hearing the life-changing voice from heaven.

## *Consider*

- If the devil can steal our affections by getting us to focus on ourselves, he will capture our desire and ensnare our will. He will entice us to walk away from God. Why?
- The key to discovering our worth is to become captivated by God. Why?
- Why did one glimpse of God's image and the sound of his voice change  every distorted self-perception within these men?

# Thirty Six

# Shine

*That you may become harmless and blameless*
*children of God without fault or blemish*
*in the midst of a crooked*
*and perverse generation*
*among who you shine as lights*
*in this world.*
(Philippians 2:15 NLT)

*R*elationship with God is a process. It never happens in one small neat encounter. Being open with God and developing a relationship with him that is strong enough for him to convince us of his love takes time, lots of time. It is the journey with him that matters, not the final destination. As we open our hearts to God and allow him to become part of our lives we will be transformed into his image. Coming into partnership with God and responding to his overtures ultimately changes us. In discovering our identity we enter into the most exciting journey of our lifetime. The presence of God within us is all we need to reflect his image. He is satisfied when we respond in a way that reveals something of his character to those around us.

The rest of the story is yours to tell as you pursue your own journey of reflecting God. He is waiting there for you in the secret place to bring you into a deep satisfying relationship with him. His heart is beating just for you. Come to him as a child. Believe he is with you. Become comfortable with his presence. Bask in the wonder of his extravagant love over your life. Allow yourself the time it takes to fall in love with God. He made you to become one in heart and spirit with him and to dance with him in the pulsating rhythm of life.

He desires to hold your hand and draw you close so you can hear his heart beating for you. He desires to walk with you within the garden of your heart. There he will gently pull out long-standing weeds of bitterness and plant, with his own hands, seeds of love that will grow and become shade to many lonely souls.

Be willing for the lover of your soul to revive the dreams you have long forgotten. Expect him to speak tenderly to your weary soul. Allow him to lift weights off your mind and redefine your image. Allow him to show you around his heart. There you will discover who you are. He wants to sing over you the many love songs he has for you alone.

Our future success lies in understanding how God sees

us. God is able to do through us far more than we think possible because only he knows what amazing qualities and abilities he has given each one of us. Living according to the way God made us, allows us to see ourselves beyond the opinion of humanity. An inner awareness of his image will be imprinted on our spirits. This image will have nothing to do with how we look, what we earn, what cool friends we have, or how much we know.

> *He is waiting there for you in the secret place to bring you into a deep satisfying relationship with him.*

In heating crude silver, the silversmith was asked how he knows when all the impurities are burned out of the silver. The silversmith replied, "It is when you can see clearly your own reflection. The clearer your reflection is, the purer the silver is."[101] God wants to see his own reflection in our lives.

By faith go into the secret place of his presence and allow God to show you around the storehouse of your identity. As you go there allow Jesus to reveal to you the intricate detail of his own nature that he has placed within you. As you reflect the essence of your new self you will mirror his image.

When you allow God to capture your heart, you will experience the deep passion that God has for you alone. Snuggle up into his arms and allow him to carry you into realms of his glory and grace. You are his mighty reflector made in his image. Shine for him.

# Notes

1      THE MESSAGE BIBLE Genesis 1:26

2      *Collins Gem English Dictionary* (Harper Collins Publishers, Glasgow Great Britain 1991, 1994, 1998, 2003) 276

3      Nelson Mandela's speech 1994

4      THE MESSAGE Ephesians 2:1

5      Craig Hill *Ancient Paths* ( Littleton: Family Foundation Publishing 1992), 13

6      THE AMPLIFIED BIBLE Proverbs 29:18

7      *Enduring words for the Athlete* (Australia: Five Mile Press Pty Ltd 2006) NP

8      Gene Edwards *The Divine Romance* (Auburn, Maine: Christian Books Publishing House, MCMLXXXIV*), 3*

9      W.E Vine *Vines Expository Dictionary* (IOWA: Riverside Book and Bible House), 587

10     *Readers Digest Oxford Complete Word Finder* (London: Readers Digest Association Limited), 740

12     THE AMPLIFIED BIBLE Song of Songs 5:10

13     THE AMPLIFIED BIBLE Revelation 1:16

14     THE MESSAGE Romans 8:31-34

15     *Funk & Wagnall Standard Desk Dictionary Revised Addition (United States of America: Funken & Wagnalls Publishing Company., Inc 1976) 452*

16     Craig Hill *Ancient Paths* ( Littleton: Family Foundation Publishing 1992), 99

17     W.E Vine *Vines Expository Dictionary* (IOWA: Riverside Book and Bible House), 264

18     THE MESSAGE Proverbs 13:2

19     *Funk & Wagnall Standard Desk Dictionary Revised Addition (United States of America: Funken & Wagnalls Publishing Company., Inc 1964, 1966, 1969, 1976*), 341.

20     *Collins Gem English Dictionary* (Harper Collins Publishers, Glasgow Great Britain 1991, 1994, 1998, 2003) 157

21     THE MESSAGE Isaiah 51:12-14

22     THE MESSAGE Isaiah 51: 14-15

23     THE MESSAGE Proverbs 15:4

24     THE MESSAGE James 3:5-8

25     THE MESSAGE Jeremiah 6:16

26      THE MESSAGE Proverbs 25:11
27      THE AMPLIFIED BIBLE Habakkuk 3:19
28      THE MESSAGE 1 Corinthians 13:12
29      THE MESSAGE 1 Corinthians 13:12
30      *Funk & Wagnall Standard Desk Dictionary Revised Addition
        (United States of America: Funken & Wagnalls Publishing Company.,
        Inc 1964, 1966, 1969, 1976)*, 727
31      W.E Vine *Vines Expository Dictionary* (IOWA: Riverside Book and
        Bible House), 186
32      ibid, 852
33      THE MESSAGE Isaiah 51:9
34      *Readers  Digest Oxford Complete Word Finder* (London: Readers
        Digest Association Limited), 1545
35      THE MESSAGE Matthew 9:35-38
36      Royee Jenson *Naked Unbelief* (Australia: City Harvest Publications
        2001), 39
37      THE AMPLIFIED BIBLE Matthew 5:5
38      Nelson Mandala *Inaugural Speech* 1994
39      THE MESSAGE Proverbs 24:10
40      *Readers Digest Oxford Complete Word Finder* (London: Readers
        Digest Association Limited),949
41      *ibid*, 949
42      *ibid*, 944
43      THE MESSAGE 2 Corinthians 6: 11-13
44      Paul Billheimer, *Destined for the Throne* (Pennsylvania: World
        Literature Crusade 1975),35
45      THE MESSAGE 2 Corinthians 7:1
46      THE MESSAGE Matthew 7: 24-25
47      W.E Vine *Vines Expository Dictionary* (IOWA: Riverside Book and
        Bible House) 132
48      THE MESSAGE Isaiah 49:17:18
49      THE MESSAGE1 Samuel 15:24
50      AW Tozer *Pursuit of God* (United Kingdom: Paternoster
        Publishing) 111 Used by permission.
51      THE MESSAGE Proverbs 16:6
52      Craig Hill *Ancient Paths* (Littleton: Family Foundation Publishing
        1992 ), 79
53      ibid 80
54      THE MESSAGE Matthew 7:12
55      THE MESSAGE Matthew 18:27

56      THE MESSAGE Matthew 5:13
57      AMPLIFIED BIBLE 1 Thessalonians 5:13-15
58      THE MESSAGE Matthew 5:13
59      THE MESSAGE Matthew 5:48
60      Source Unknown
61      THE MESSAGE Proverbs 14:12-13
62      W.E Vine *Vines Expository Dictionary* (IOWA: Riverside Book and
        Bible House) 493
63      W.E Vine *Vines Expository Dictionary* (IOWA: Riverside Book and
        Bible House), 1054
64      ibid 1054
65      THE MESSAGE Galatians 5:16-18
66      THE MESSAGE Romans 8:8
67      Hannah Hurnard *Kingdom of Love* (Wheaton, Illinois: Tyndale House
        Publishers, Inc 1976), 58
68      W.E Vine *Vines Expository Dictionary* (IOWA: Riverside Book and
        Bible House ), 135
69      THE MESSAGE Galatians 5:22-23
70      W.E Vine *Vines Expository Dictionary* (IOWA: Riverside Book and
        Bible House ) 1066
71      THE MESSAGE 2 Corinthians 6:17-18
72      THE MESSAGE James 4:4-6
73      THE MESSAGE Matthew 11:28
74      THE MESSAGE Galatians 3:5
75      THE MESSAGE 2 Corinthians 6:16-18
76      Ian McCormack Campbelltown Catholic Club 13 July, 2003
77      THE MESSAGE Isaiah 49: 15-16
78      THE MESSAGE Galatians 4:7-10
79      THE MESSAGE Matthew 6:6
80      A.W. Tozer *Pursuit of God* (United Kingdom: Paternoster
        Publishing), 17.
81      THE MESSAGE Psalm 34:5
82      AW Tozer *Pursuit of God* (United Kingdom: Paternoster
        Publishing),17
83      ibid 13
84      THE AMPLIFIED BIBLE Psalm 91:1
85      THE MESSAGE Psalm 18:24
86      THE MESSAGE Proverbs 3:6
87      A.W. Tozer *Pursuit of God* (United Kingdom: Paternoster

Publishing),108

88     A.J. Russell *GOD CALLING* (Australia: W.A. Buchanan & Co, 1953 sixth addition 2001), 40

89     *Readers Digest Oxford Complete Word Finder* (London: Readers Digest Association Limited ), 902

90     AW Tozer *Pursuit of God* (United Kingdom: Paternoster Publishing), 89

91     W.E Vine *Vines Expository Dictionary* (IOWA: Riverside Book and Bible House), 586

92     Campbelltown Catholic Club 13 July 2001

93     THE MESSAGE Romans 8:6-8

94     THE MESSAGE Matthew 10:29-31

95     THE MESSAGE Romans 8:16

96     *Enduring Words for the Athlete* (Australia: Five Mile Press Pty Ltd 2006)

97     THE MESSAGE Proverbs 14:26

98     THE MESSAGE Proverbs 14:27

99     *The Concise Oxford Dictionary* Oxford University Press, (ENSHU BUILDING, OTSUKA, BUNKYO-KU, TOKYO, 1964), 426

100   THE MESSAGE Proverbs 13:9

101   Source Unknown

102   Cooke, Graham *The Language of Promise* (Kent, England: Sovereign World 2004), 37